CHILDREN AND DISASTERS

CHILDREN AND DISASTERS
A Practical Guide to Healing and Recovery

EDITED BY

Wendy N. Zubenko, ED.D., M.S.N., R.N., C.S.
UNIVERSITY OF PITTSBURGH MEDICAL CENTER
WESTERN PSYCHIATRIC INSTITUTE & CLINIC

Joseph Capozzoli, R.N.
THE JOHNS HOPKINS UNIVERSITY

OXFORD
UNIVERSITY PRESS

2002

OXFORD

UNIVERSITY PRESS

Oxford   New York
Auckland   Bangkok   Buenos Aires   Cape Town   Chennai
Dar es Salaam   Delhi   Hong Kong   Istanbul   Karachi   Kolkata
Kuala Lumpur   Madrid   Melbourne   Mexico City   Mumbai   Nairobi
São Paulo   Shanghai   Singapore   Taipei   Tokyo   Toronto

and an associated company in Berlin

Copyright © 2002 by Oxford University Press

Published by Oxford University Press, Inc.
198 Madison Avenue, New York, New York 10016
www.oup.com

Oxford is a registered trademark of Oxford University Press

Library of Congress Cataloging-in-Publication Data
Children and disasters : a practical guide to healing and recovery / edited by Wendy N.
Zubenko, Joseph Capozzoli.
    p. cm.
  ISBN 0-19-513573-3; 0-19-515490-8 (pbk.)
    1. Child disaster victims—Mental health—Handbooks, manuals, etc. 2. Disasters—
Psychological aspects—Handbooks, manuals, etc. 3. Crisis intervention. (Mental health
services)—Handbooks, manuals, etc. 4. Post-traumatic stress disorder in children—
Handbooks, manuals, etc. I. Zubenko, Wendy N., 1962– II. Capozzoli, Joseph. 1953–

RJ507.D57 C485 2002
618.92'8521—dc21   2002016973

9 8 7 6 5 4 3 2 1

Printed in the United States of America
on acid-free paper

To Mathieu, Niki, Natalie, and Christopher. I'll always be
here for you.

—W.N.Z.

To Melissa, Michele, and Jeff . . . all my love always.

—J.A.C.

Preface

SEPTEMBER 11, 2001, WILL FOREVER BE REMEMBERED AS THE day that the world as we know it changed forever. The terrorist attacks on the World Trade Center and the Pentagon and the thwarted attempt to attack a second location in Washington, D.C., brought the world to a standstill. The majority of the world community shares in our feelings of shock, devastation, and grief. For many, especially our children, this has become a very frightening and unsafe world. At the last count nearly 3,000 people from 80 different nations lost their lives as they went about their daily routines. Our loss included hundreds of brave New York firefighters, paramedics, and police officers who were trying to help and rescue victims. Countless numbers of children have lost at least one parent; corporations have lost their employees; many battalions lost a significant number of firefighters; families and communities have been shattered by the loss of mothers, fathers, sons, daughters, sisters, brothers, friends, uncles, aunts, cousins, nieces, nephews, grandparents, grandchildren, and other dearly loved ones.

But even in this time of great national (worldwide) tragedy and mourning, there are daily reminders of the goodness and strength in others. The outpouring of offers of help and assistance not only from every community in the United States but also from around the world was tremendous. Immediately, agencies such as the American Red Cross and the Salvation Army activated their disaster plans and began the arduous task of helping the individuals, communities, and nation to recover. The recovery efforts will take a very long time. Disaster relief efforts will be needed for years to come. The psychological impact on all of us, but most especially on our children, will be huge and long-standing. We hope that this manual will serve as a guide as we all help our children through this unthinkable tragedy and assist them in integrating these experiences, developing healthy coping skills, and becoming stronger people.

Wendy Nuss Zubenko
Joseph Capozzoli

Contents

About the Editors and Contributors   xi

Introduction   3

**1   Psychological Relief: An Overview—
The Balkan Experience**
Joseph Capozzoli   6

**2   Disaster Mental Health:
Trauma Relief, Concepts, and Theory**
John D. Weaver   34

**3   Understanding Children in Crisis:
The Developmental Ecological Framework**
Wanda K. Mohr   72

4   Developmental Issues in Stress and Crisis
Wendy N. Zubenko   85

5   Post Traumatic Stress Disorder and Reaction
June A. Esser   101

6   The Role of Play in the Recovery Process
Carol M. Raynor   124

7   Group Interventions for Children in Crisis
*Gordana Kuterovac Jagodic, Ksenija Kontac,
and Wendy N. Zubenko*   135

8   Normalization: A Key to Children's Recovery
Gordana Kuterovac Jagodic and Ksenija Kontac   159

Index   173

About the Editors and Contributors

The Editors

Wendy N. Zubenko is Clinical Nurse Specialist and Program Coordinator for the Molecular Neurobiology and Genetics Laboratory at the University of Pittsburgh. She has extensive experience with trauma and crisis mental health with people across the lifespan from young children through geriatrics, and worked for many years in a psychiatric emergency room.

Joseph A. Capozzoli is a psychiatric mental health nurse in the Division of Child Psychiatry and Adolescent Psychiatry at the Johns Hopkins Hospital in Baltimore, Maryland. He has extensive clinical experience with children in various settings, and has worked internationally caring for children who were displaced by the war in the Balkans.

The Contributors

June A. Esser, M.S.N., R.N., C.S.
Clinical Nurse Specialist
University of Pittsburgh Medical Center
Pittsburgh, PA
Private Practice
Center for Creative Living
Fox Chapel, Pennsylvania

Gordana Kuterovac Jagodic, Ph.D
Department of Psychology
Faculty of Philosophy
University of Zagreb, Croatia

Ksenija Kontac, Ph.D.
Society for Psychological Assistance
Zagreb, Croatia

Wanda K. Mohr, Ph.D., R.N., F.A.A.N.
Associate Professor
Psychiatric Mental Health Nursing
Indiana University
Purdue University
Indianapolis, Indiana

Carol M. Raynor, M.S.N., R.N., C.S.
Clinical Therapist
Butterfield Youth Services
Marshall, Missouri

John D. Weaver, LCSW, ACSW, BCD
Northampton County Mental Health/Mental Retardation
Private Practice
Eye of the Storm, Inc.
Nazareth, Pennsylvania

CHILDREN AND DISASTERS

Introduction

Disasters and trauma (whether natural or man-made) leave deep emotional scars on children and adolescents. Helping these youngsters in the healing process is a bit of a departure from the routine, traditional work of mental health professionals. Psychiatrists, psychologists, nurses, social workers, and other professionals receive little or no formal training in disaster mental health relief. The small amount of training that is available is usually more theoretical in nature and often does not include practical aspects of providing care.

This book provides readers with both the practical and theoretical principles that they need to consider when providing relief for victims (especially children) of trauma and widespread disasters.

Chapter 1 by Joseph Capozolli introduces the reader to the fundamental concepts that are used in large-scale relief efforts. Capozzoli draws on his experiences in the Balkans to give practical examples and provide ideas for interventions that can be used in many settings.

In chapter 2, John D. Weaver, a longtime member of the American Red Cross's Disaster Mental Health Team, focuses on

3

the concepts and theories of trauma relief. He presents basic disaster mental health (DMH) terms and concepts, describes the phases of reaction and recovery, and discusses the common feelings and reactions experienced by most victims of trauma and disaster. Key DMH guidelines and interventions are discussed in detail.

In chapter 3 Wanda K. Mohr provides a theoretical framework from which we can approach the psychological relief efforts for children and adolescents. This chapter presents a theoretical perspective that describes the complexity that we face in understanding the interplay of biology, psychology, social, and cultural forces, all of which must be taken into account when considering a child in crisis.

Wendy N. Zubenko addresses developmental issues in stress and crisis in chapter 4. This chapter reviews normal child and adolescent development and describes children's responses to traumatic events based on their developmental level. The chapter discusses warning signs that a child's usual way of coping is no longer working or is unhealthy. Specific interventions are also discussed.

Chapter 5 focuses on posttraumatic stress in children. June A. Esser, explores posttraumatic stress disorder (PTSD) and posttraumatic stress reaction (PTSR) in youths exposed to catastrophic events. Esser focuses on wellness promotion in interventions and approaches intervention in a holistic manner that incorporates the will, the imagination, the intellect, and the physical, psychological, and spiritual aspects of a person.

In chapter 6 Carol Raynor discusses the important role of play in the process of trauma recovery. She provides very practical, easy-to-implement interventions that can be incorporated into any setting.

Group interventions for children in crisis is the focus of chapter 7. Group activities serve many purposes, such as organizing the children's time; providing a comforting and supportive environment; promoting healthy expression of thoughts and feelings that encourage socialization; and providing opportunities for building confidence, skills, and knowledge. This chapter was co-written by Gordana Kuterovac Jagodic, Ksenija Kontac, and Wendy N. Zubenko. (Jagodic is a faculty member in the Department of Psychology, Faculty of Philosophy at the University of Zagreb, Croatia. Kontac works for the Society for Psychological Assistance in Zagreb, Croatia.)

The ultimate goal of psychological relief for children is normalization, the subject of the last chapter. In chapter 8 Jagodic and Kontak discuss the goal of early interventions for children after a crisis, and as the authors point out, trauma workers should target activities that return normalcy—normalization of daily life and the normalization of reactions and symptoms. They describe in detail their own experiences and provide specific interventions that help to normalize a child's disrupted and often chaotic world.

Psychological Relief

AN OVERVIEW: THE BALKAN EXPERIENCE

Joseph A. Capozzoli

INDIVIDUALS LIKE TO BE ABLE TO PREDICT, FORESEE, AND IN-fluence events. When we are placed in situations in which we are powerless and unable to influence events, we become victims. Disastrous and devastating events, especially those events that are unpredicted, are the spawning ground for psychological trauma. Indeed, very serious psychological repercussions can result in individuals who have been exposed to trauma which stems from displacement from home, death of loved ones, loss of community, and an inability to predict the future with any degree of certainty. There are many causes of psychological trauma, some more overt than others and easier to understand. Despite our level of understanding, few instances evoke more sympathy and concern than that of a child who is suffering, regardless of the cause.

Over the past several decades, scientific and technological advances have revolutionized the way we treat and care for the mentally ill. During this same period we have also learned a great deal about those who have suffered from the traumas of war, earthquakes, flooding, plane crashes, and other types of disasters. These tragic experiences have yielded many valuable lessons about the principles of providing psychological assistance. This chapter provides the framework and acquaints the reader with necessary background information needed to deliver psychological relief to trauma victims.

The interrelationship of professionals, lead agencies, and local workers in disaster relief efforts are vital to the ongoing success of any program. Cultural sensitivity, the role of the media, the nature of interventions, and means of measuring outcomes are all discussed. The chapter sets the stage for topics that are presented in greater detail later in the book. These topics include but are not limited to debriefing, individual differences within a traumatized population, and the "normal response" to trauma.

THE ORIGIN OF PSYCHOLOGICAL TRAUMA

Unfortunately, there are many events that can impart devastating physical and psychological trauma on individuals. These events fall under two main categories: man-made (those we bring on ourselves) and natural disasters. Man-made disasters include war, terrorism, violence, torture, sacrifice, and other human acts that create mayhem. The war in the Balkans during the early 1990s contained all of these elements and affected the population of two countries. Men, women, and children of all ages were traumatized by constant terror over a 5-year period. The conflict continues intermittently today.

During the Balkan conflict more than 385,000 people were displaced from their families. Approximately 32% of those displaced were children and adolescents (Adjukovic, 1994). Displacement can cause a multitude of problems, including financial difficulties, the breakdown of the social network, social isolation, a marginalized status, uncertainty about the future, and mental trauma. Multiple losses, such as the death of family members and displacement from home, intensify mental health problems and accentuate problems associated with displacement.

Unfortunately, war is not the only source of modern trauma. In the United States firearms have posed an equally devastating threat to our children. In recent years parents, professionals, and many others, including children, have become more concerned about the impact of firearms on our society. The American Academy of Child and Adolescent Psychiatry ("Facts for Families," 1992) published the following:

- Every day 10 American children aged 18 and under are killed in handgun suicides, homicides, or accidents. Many more are wounded.
- Gunshot wounds to children have increased 300% in major urban areas since 1986.
- 60% of teen deaths by suicide involve the use of a gun. Nearly 3,000 teens use handguns to commit suicide every year.
- An estimated 400,000 youngsters carried handguns to school in 1987. In Baltimore, half of the males have reported taking a gun to high school.

It is easy to understand why adults often have an strong response to these data. What about children and adolescents? How safe do they feel?

A 5-year-old kindergartner is killed in a drive-by shooting, and the tragedy attracts significant media attention. But after the story fades from the headlines in a day or two, no one hears about what happens to the rest of the school children who have lost a classmate. Whether the violence, loss, grief, and tragedy occurs in our own backyard or in Croatia, at Columbine High

School, or in the streets of New York, Washington, and Pennsylvania, the issues remain the same. Families are broken apart, parents are dead or missing, neighborhoods and schools are no longer safe havens. Many of our children are, sadly, refugees in their own homes and communities.

One of my colleagues and I are beginning to look at how this stress and trauma are affecting children in school. We are now beginning to see a group of children who have developed a fear of school—not because of an anxiety disorder but because they are afraid to go to school, where they might get killed (Joshi, 1996).

In addition to the trauma we bring on ourselves, natural disasters can traumatize a population. Individuals can suffer from psychological trauma secondary to fire, earthquakes, flooding, and other disasters. We have all witnessed the physical effects of natural disasters on the evening news. In recent years we have seen entire segments of our country devastated by flooding. Recently several hundred thousand people died and even more were left homeless after a major earthquake in Iran.

Whether the disaster is an act of nature or an act of man, the psychological trauma that occurs can be equally devastating. Galante and Foa (1986) found that children exhibited a wide range of behaviors in response to an earthquake that occurred in a rural mountain region in central Italy. Children were described as apathetic, aggressive, and at times even assaultive. In short, their behavior was characterized as being extreme and exaggerated. These children had been subjected to death and loss of home and belongings, and they were living in unrecognizable traces of their homes and villages. In their now-shattered world they manifested severe behavior problems which added to the difficulties of a community ravaged by nature.

Interventions need to occur soon after a traumatizing event. Long-term, severe complications may develop if psychological interventions are delayed. Bowlby (1973) and others have found that children who suffer from the loss of a loved one or care-taker are more apt to develop emotional or personality distur-bances than children who have not. He went on to state that children's difficulties are often overlooked or minimized while the adults in the family respond to the loss. These rebuffed and otherwise unaddressed feelings can often catalyze other prob-lems which occur long after the event. Howard and Gordon (1972) followed San Francisco earthquake victims for 1 year after that catastrophe. Although immediate counseling and com-munity outreach were effective in most cases, some of the vic-tims continued to have symptoms beyond the 1-year period counselors often monitor. Regardless of how or why the trauma occurred, professionals must remain keenly aware and sensitive to the needs of children and adolescents during the wake of any disaster. All of these traumatic events can interfere with normal psychological development.

THE FIRST STEP IN PROVIDING RELIEF: LISTEN

Our natural human impulse is to ask "Why?" to try to under-stand the genesis of disasters. However, it is important in our relief efforts to understand the immediate needs of victims. A few years back I found myself in Slunj, a small town in Croatia on the Bosnian border. As I looked around I kept asking myself, "How did this happen?" I was horrified at the events that were described to me by our escorts. Our team spent countless hours debriefing because of the sights that we witnessed. We empa-thized and bonded with those who suffered. But it was only after we overcame our own feelings that we were able to help provide relief for others.

One day I spoke at length with an older woman who was caring for her infant grandson. We "spoke" by using hand signs and drawing pictures in the sand in front of her demolished home. I learned that her son was helping to dig a grave for his wife, who had been killed in a recent raid on the town. We struggled with our primitive communication for about 45 minutes until my escort arrived and assisted with translation. The old woman showed me her ravaged home and invited me in. Inside her home was a makeshift table, the fireplace in which she cooked food, and the bed that she shared with her son and grandson. She went on to describe how the soldiers arrived, drove people from their homes, and then destroyed everything. They deliberately ravaged the town so that the remaining townspeople were unable to occupy their homes. I was numb from her story but continued to talk with her through our translator. She said that I reminded her of a friend. We hugged goodbye, but I was left feeling that I should have done more. I shared my feelings with our team during the ride back to Zagreb and re-iterated my desire to help this woman. A Croatian psychologist who was driving the van smiled. He looked over at me and said, "You have helped." I looked puzzled, and he continued, "That is the first time she has spoken to anyone about what happened to her. Her healing has begun."

It is more important for victims to be able to talk about what happened to them than it is for providers to understand why it happened. It is equally important for victims to feel that they are being listened to by people who really hear them, and who care. We can measure the success of our relief efforts by our understanding of how the victims feel, as opposed to our understanding of the events themselves, which may remain inexplicable in their randomness and callousness. Listening, hearing, and showing care and compassion become even more important when working with children. Carl Taylor (1996) recounts an interaction that he had with a child in India that exemplifies how disasters and tragedies affect children:

Alma was a little girl about twelve years old. As we were finishing up the afternoon's work I chose her for the last examination. It was very difficult to get her to start talking, but halfway through the screening test she opened up when given a chance to describe what had happened to her. The story flooded out about her father and brothers being machine gunned down in front of her and her mother while they hid in the tall grass. She went on about how they had to flee their home when it was being burned down by their neighbors. As we finished the test she asked shyly if she could ask a question, "Is it all right to talk about what I have seen?" In response to my little speech about not only being all right but positively beneficial to get all of her experiences and worries out so they could be discussed realistically, she said how all the adults in her life had been telling her to stop talking about her troubles, and I find this over and over again.

The normal human response, of parents and adults, is generally to tell their children, "Forget it. Don't talk about it. It is over." But it is not over. They keep saying this kind of thing over and over, "Don't think about the past, only think about the future." And Alma said with tears, "I can't forget my father and brothers." I stayed and chatted with her. I took the time for a short session of counseling. The remarkable resilience of children seemed evident as she left the room. Her face was totally changed. She was radiant and she went out saying, "I am going to organize a secret discussion group with my friends so that I can share with them what you have told me."

We can all hypothesize about ways to avoid future disasters, but this is of little use to those who have been traumatized. We need to let the victims speak out about what is important to them. We need to listen and provide the children with a safe haven in which to speak. Although it is certainly natural to ask questions, we must caution ourselves against being so drawn into the event that we lose sight of our mission. If we are to be agents of change and assistance, then we should view history through the eyes of those for whom we wish to provide relief.

THOSE WHO RESPOND, THOSE WHO SUSTAIN

There are several groups of individuals who are responsible for the success of psychological intervention in the wake of a disaster. Three distinct groups—the lead agency, the disaster relief team; and the local relief team—are discussed in this section.

Lead Agency

The lead agency is responsible for getting the relief workers access to a particular area. Agencies such as the Red Cross (RC), Catholic Relief Services (CRS), and United States Agency for International Development (USAID) are examples of lead agencies. These organizations provide access, administrative support, and in some instances coordination of relief efforts. They assist professionals and trained workers to gain access to an area or a population in need of assistance which would ordinarily be closed to them. These lead agencies play a vital role in the structure and implementation of a psychological relief effort. The work done by our team in Croatia during the Balkan crisis was coordinated by CRS and the Society for Psychological Assistance (SPA). Through these agencies we were able to gain access to areas of the country that would have otherwise been prohibited. In addition, we were able to coordinate our efforts with professionals already involved in that region. The lead agencies are usually politically neutral and widely recognized as organizations with a positive reputation for assistance in difficult situations. They are often embraced by a local population and not questioned as to their presence and motives.

The Response Team

The second group of individuals make up the response team. This group generally comprises mental health professionals who have been trained in providing psychological relief. This group is often referred to as trainers. The members of this team usually include nurses, psychologists, social workers, psychiatrists, and, in some instances, teachers. The primary purpose of this team is to work with local professionals in training others who can continue relief efforts after the response team leaves an area. The response team may work with individual victims or, as is most often the case, provide training and develop local programs that will change as the population begins to recover.

No matter how large or small the tragic event, the response team should always be coordinated by the lead agency. Extensive planning is an integral part of providing relief to coordinate efforts and to maximize the use of resources. The most well-meaning individuals soon find themselves powerless and without resources unless a lead agency guides their efforts. The communication between the lead agency and the response team must be clear and consistent so that the goals remain well defined to all.

The response team usually has a time-limited function. It is, however, vital to the success of any project that the efforts of the response team continue to be carried out by the community once the team has left. Psychological responses to disasters can be devastating to individuals in an acute phase, but these responses may also persist over time, sometimes years after the disaster. Relief efforts should have a component capable of sustaining efforts over a long period. Because the response team is generally a group visiting an area, it is vital that training of local individuals takes place so that interventions may be carried on over time.

The Local Relief Team

The third group, the local relief team, is made up of individuals who are part of a geographic area or part of an extended relief effort. This group can include a variety of people who are able to have extended contact with individuals and populations who have been victimized by the disaster. These individuals come from all walks of life and have been trained in psychological relief by professionals, typically the response team. This group helps provide the other members of the team with necessary information about the culture and mores of the victims. The local relief team is better able to recruit and stress the importance of programs that include community groups and victims. In the best scenario, the local group begins to function as a response team and begins to spawn an effort that reaches well beyond the initial scope of the lead agency. These local relief agents provide the ongoing work that will endure long after the initial relief interventions are completed.

PSYCHOLOGICAL ASSISTANCE, NOT PSYCHOTHERAPY

The model that relief workers should employ is one of assistance, not therapy. It is important that professionals view individuals as victims, not patients or clients. I have often heard the following observation: "The day before this event happened, these folks were just like you and me." The children in Croatia, New York, Washington, D.C., and Pennsylvania clearly illustrate this point. These children were attending school, living at home, playing sports, and involved in recreational activities with their peers and, suddenly, they were traumatized by acts of death and destruction. The communities in which they lived were forever changed, and life as it was yesterday no longer exists. For these children the stressors were acute: Many had lost significant loved ones; some had witnessed traumatic events while fleeing; some were living with distressed adults; some had lost educational opportunities; and some were now in poor, unsanitary, and sometimes unsafe living conditions. Natural disasters such as earthquakes and flooding often bring on similar types of stressors.

For the children of Croatia, the most frequent and common psychological disturbances were weeping, nightmares, bedwetting, tics, aggressive behavior, and general withdrawal (Dzepina et al., 1992). Parents' reactions and behaviors are the main mediator that can contribute to or alleviate the effects of stress on a child's development (Garbarino, 1991). Efforts cannot be confined to "traditional" therapeutic approaches but need to encompass the child's entire living situation. Involving families and communities is an integral part of providing a healing social network for children. Community involvement is also an effective way to reduce the stigma of a victim in society. Those who have suffered and who have been able to become part of a social network or group are less apt to be viewed in a negative way by others.

A child's developmental stage can pose particular difficulties when facing trauma and stress. Anyone who has worked with children knows that they can be very unreliable when asked "How do you feel?" They will tell us what they think we want to hear, what they understand, what others have told them, but they will seldom say, "I don't really understand your question." If, however, we explain to children that it is okay to feel the way they do, we will gain much more insight into how they are feeling. The model used with children in the refugee camps in Croatia was one of community-based activities as opposed to one of traditional psychotherapy.

Psychiatric approaches that emphasize individual problems and treatments are not helpful in these settings. Emphasis on groups, family, and community is an effective way to normalize a child's environment and to give children and adults the social support they need during the crisis. In addition, group, family, and community work is an effective and efficient way to address the often large numbers of individuals affected by traumatic events, especially given the limited resources associated with relief efforts. Parties, sports activities, dances, crafts, and group recreation were used in the refugee camps of Croatia to get refugees more involved in education, training, and regular health checkups. This community-based model was useful in creating a longitudinal approach that was able to meet the changing needs of the population (Adjukovic & Ljuubotina, 1995). Normalizing a child's environment is so crucial to the success of psychological assistance that an entire chapter of this book has been devoted to it (see chapter 8). Normalization is indeed the key to recovery. Community-based programs are also more apt to endure the test of time and are particularly useful when working with children and adolescents who need a network of support.

From a developmental perspective, the needs of children and adolescents change over time. Community-based programs have the ability to evolve with the changing needs of a population. In much the same way in which a school setting changes from Grade 1 to Grade 12, groups can change as the needs of the members become different. Therefore, an approach which is sensitive to change is better suited to meet the needs of this population across a developmental continuum.

CULTURAL SENSITIVITY

Like so many other terms in social science, *culture* is a difficult concept to define. As used by anthropologists, the term means the totality of practices, artifacts, customs, taboos, and mores that characterize a given group living in a more or less circumscribed place. As a society grows more sophisticated and worldly, any description of its culture becomes increasingly complex. In a country such as the United States, with its multitudes of subcultures from all over the world, the concept of an "American culture" can sometimes be an abstraction with fuzzy edges. Each individual is a unique creation, and heredity, family constellation, economic level, and experience all make their contributions to that individual's "culture." The historical period in which an individual is born, the geographical place in which he or she grows up, and chance or fate all participate in his or her uniqueness (Elkind & Weiner, 1972).

Despite the growing literature on cultural sensitivity, the importance of culture is often overlooked when providing psychological relief to individuals. How do we become more sensitive to culture? Often, being immersed in the culture helps, as does working side by side with the local relief team. When I was visiting Croatia I was surprised when I did not see Halloween treats and carved pumpkins. But I quickly learned that All Hallow's Eve and All Saints' Day were very different kinds of celebrations that involved family dinner and the visiting of gravesites of departed family members. Recognition of the relevance of this particular holiday played an integral part in subsequent conversations between relief workers and the refugee population. The customs that surrounded this holiday became the basis for discussions in the days and even weeks that followed the actual event. Refugees were more apt to discuss events during this time because it was customary to do so. The fabric of the society had a season already built into its framework which allowed and encouraged its members to talk, to grieve, and to reflect on the passing of loved ones. It is crucial for us as relief workers to gain an understanding of what is important, considered "normal," and accepted for the population we are serving.

Interestingly, groups gathered in churches, that they hadn't frequented prior to the holiday. In these settings communities were able to set aside some of the ethnic bias that had spawned the conflict initially. Indeed, the focus of an entire culture was on those who had passed away. In some of the communities that were devastated by bombing, large-scale efforts were undertaken to get their churches ready for the holiday season. In the midst of all this activity refugees became more active in their own healing process. Parents conversed more with their children, and the atmosphere was less guarded with respect to those who had died and those who were missing. This was not just another holiday, but the start of a new beginning for many.

Cultural sensitivity should not be confined to international relief work. In our own country cultural barriers exist within and between different communities. Table 1.1 lists some of the differences within the population demographics found in the United States that suggest the presence of cultural, geographical, educational, and family differences in our society. Cultural diversity needs to be identified and considered when a person. community, or region is the object of a relief effort.

Even within one state, the differences between urban and suburban adolescents can be just some of the demographic variables to consider. Brown (1986) found that low income urban adolescents experienced a significantly higher number of negative events than did suburban adolescents. Opie et al. (1992) suggests that the number of deaths experienced by this population over a 2-year period may be as high as 60% and that very little is known about the grieving process for this group. This kind of statistic illustrates that even with a population parameter, such as age, differences exist both in the exposure to events and with regard to information and resources available to individuals who may need intervention.

If one were to travel around the United States, it would become apparent that different regions have their own local flavor. Comfort levels and sensitivity to events, although not readily apparent, exist within a local population. For example, if one were to examine the clothing of individuals in a metropolitan area, diversity would certainly be a factor. Furthermore, if an individual were suddenly removed from a metropolitan setting and placed in a more rural environment, the difference in dress would be immediately evident. In addition, a certain stigma would be attached to an individual who did not conform to the local customs. The situation would be a strain for both the dis-

TABLE 1.1.
Population Comparisons in the United States

	1990	2000
Resident population (in millions)	248.8	281.4
Percent of population under 18 years old	25.7%	26%
Race (percent)		
White	74.9%	70.7%
Black	12.3%	12.3%
Asian or Pacific Islander	3.0%	3.6%
American Indian/Eskimo	0.8%	0.9%
Hispanic	9.0%	12.5%
Metropolitan area residents (in millions)	79.7	82
Families		
Married families (in millions)	66.1	71
Married with children under 18 (in millions)	32.3	35.1
Percentage of one-parent homes	24%	31.6%
Education (persons 25 years old and older)		
High school graduate	77.6%	83.1%
College graduate	21.3%	24.9%

Note. Data are from U.S. Bureau of Census (2000).

placed individual and the local population. These differences are magnified in the wake of a disaster.

The flooding in the Midwest over the past decade caused a great number of individuals to be displaced forced to change their residences. Moving a family and possessions is stressful under the best of circumstances. When unplanned and coupled with life-threatening conditions, trauma can easily result. Suddenly without a home or community, customs and life patterns are altered without warning, and many find themselves living in an unfamiliar area with its own customs very different from their own. The Midwest experience was complicated by the fact that individuals were not always able to carry their identities with them. They were not viewed as what they once were but as what they had become—victims. They were no longer local factory workers, little league coaches, politicians, shopkeepers, or community activists; they were victims of a disaster, and they were homeless.

Psychological relief efforts for displaced populations need to incorporate a delicate balance, linking past experiences and accomplishments with assimilation into a new environment. The distinct cultural differences of a population and the nature of the disastrous event make each situation unique. It is of little use to bring preconceived notions or an agenda into planning or taking part in a relief effort. The importance of the local relief team has previously been described, but it is helpful to elaborate on its unique function in view of the cultural diversity that we often encounter. The local relief team, because of geographical proximity, is better able to identify the needs of the affected population. The local team is also most likely skilled at determining the types of interventions that will be most helpful in providing relief services for the target population. These local team members are aware of the normal grief process and mechanisms that may be already in place to help a particular population. Relief workers going to a different country or region that has been affected by a disaster are at a distinct disadvantage if they are unable to collaborate with a local relief team. In the Balkans, for example, local relief teams not only provided international teams with cultural information but also served as translators who were fluent in local dialects. The Society for Psychological Assistance (SPA) had many local teams in various regions who were able to identify specific needs based on the cultural differences of each population of refugees, which were distinct throughout the war-torn country. It was clear from the outset that any campaign for relief would have to incorporate these individuals in order to be successful.

If a local relief team is not in place, it is important to begin to establish one as soon as possible. Local U.S. agencies such as the YMCA (Young Men's Christian Association), Veterans of Foreign Wars (VFW) posts, Elks lodges, and the like are good places to start. Local chapters of the Red Cross and local social service agencies can be instrumental in creating avenues and providing information for relief workers internationally. These organizations, although they may not have the expertise, have already organized a collection of community-oriented individuals who would welcome support from external groups.

THE MEDIA

There is much debate about the media and their role in the United States. Violence in the media, the definition of pornography, advertisements, censorship, and control are just some of these controversial hot-button topics. The media, especially television, are often viewed negatively, and we have even adopted some common phrases such as "boob tube" to indicate our collective disdain. Radio, newspapers, and magazines are viewed in a somewhat more positive manner, but the scope of what they provide for us is limited.

The media are included in this discussion not to continue the debate over their uses and abuses but to demonstrate how they can be used effectively by relief workers. The media are powerful. And so we must learn to embrace them but to help them focus. Relief workers and organizations have a responsibility to educate and direct the media with regard to the needs of a population—what has been done, and what still needs to be done in order to meet the needs of the victims. This is especially true in providing psychological relief. Occasionally the media provide the general population with pictures, stories, and contact numbers of organizations that are offering medical supplies, food, and shelter for victims. Psychological relief efforts, however, are seldom reported or identified, and therefore they remain beyond the realm of what the general public is apprised of by the media. Although relief workers need to be very guarded and sensitive about overpublicizing the plight of traumatized individuals, they must also find avenues to promote their work. The publicizing of conferences, workshops, and related events is an excellent way to get more general coverage. A few years ago I did a presentation at a colloquium on violence and psychological relief, hosted by the Children's Center at the Johns Hopkins Hospital. The event was attended by international experts, local experts, law enforcement officials, politicians, and leaders of the Red Cross and Catholic Relief Services. During the discussions it became apparent that this would have been an excellent event for the media to cover, but they were not invited. It was agreed by all the participants that any such future event would include the media so that relief efforts could begin to become more widely recognized by the general public. It was a valuable lesson learned by all.

Publicity comes in many forms, and the general public is often responsive to novel approaches in reporting events. For example, a school in a small Croatian border town called Slunj had been dismantled and used to house enemy soldiers during the war. When the armies left, they made sure that all the heating and plumbing in the structure were destroyed. They also attempted to burn all the books and educational materials they could find. When I met a teacher from this school, she was in the process of trying to put the school back together for the few children that had returned to the town. She told our team how she always tried to listen to the radio each day to stay in touch with the world from her war-torn home. One day, as she was listening to a talk show, she heard the broadcaster saying that all the refugees were finally returning to their homes and getting their lives back together. He went on to say how they were returning to their original homes and how wonderful it was that they would soon be able to be in their own communities again. As she looked out of her own window, the teacher saw homes that were totally destroyed, families living in makeshift structures, very few children, and no community. She immediately took pen in hand and began composing her own set of lyrics to the national anthem of Croatia. She vividly described how the families were returning to nothing. She wrote about the destruction and devastation and the impossible task of trying to rebuild while still under the threat of sniper fire and occasional "unsanctioned raids." She spoke about the unexploded mines and the lack of electricity, water, and medical facilities. She called the radio station and sang her song on the air. And moments after, the station was flooded with calls about the song and requests to play it again. People wanted to know how to contact her, and several groups wanted to give their support. She had harnessed the media. Her act, initially spawned by outrage, put the "real issues" before a massive public forum. Much can be learned from her courageous act.

The media must be made aware of the complex issues surrounding any event that they are covering and must report the facts accurately. One of the dimensions of any relief effort is publicity, and it must be harnessed for the good. The following are some suggested guidelines for publicizing events that involve psychological relief work.

- **Remain sensitive.** Due to the personal devastation that often accompanies these types of events, every effort must be undertaken to protect the rights and privacy of victims.
- **Avoid sensationalism.** The facts concerning these events are more than adequate to suggest the nature of the problems at hand. Melodrama rings false in the face of tragedy.
- **Communicate with agencies.** It is important and often helpful to communicate your plans, ideas, and intentions to all involved. If, for example, you are a member of a response team, you should communicate media involvement with the lead agency, as well as the local team. The various teams may be able to provide a particular slant to your story. They may have an agenda that you could help with, or they may be able to provide you with new and related information. It is also worth remembering that your actions are probably being sanctioned by a large organization that needs to be made aware of these types of issues!
- **Talk to your audience.** If you are addressing the general public, then it is not useful to present them with scientific data. Likewise, if your venue is an academic publication, factual data will probably speak louder than raw emotion.
- **Look for opportunities.** Whenever possible, use the media to engage the broader population and solicit its aid and raise its awareness. If possible, ask for a draft of the news story or press release.

The media are not always interested in reporting the stories of the victims and the relief efforts, but they usually follow a lead or try to cover an event if they believe it is important. Help them understand the tragedy of the event and how they can help in reporting the facts.

EVALUATION

In every field of study, much can be gained from empirical work. The essence of what one does, how it is done, and how others react to it is much more relevant when it can be operationalized. When particular activities are well defined, they are more easily followed by others. The realm of psychological disaster, although not exactly new, has been studied more closely in recent times. The recipes for success in this relatively young field of study are very useful templates for recovery teams to implement when engaging in relief efforts.

Traditional researchers start with a hypothesis, collect data, examine the data, and then make statements as to whether or not the data are supportive of the hypothesis. But traditional research, even in its most simplistic form, poses certain obstacles for those who provide psychological relief to victims of trauma or disaster who wish to follow up their interventions with research into their effectiveness. This section provides the reader with some suggestions about how to collect data under adverse conditions, such as those encountered in relief efforts.

Sensitivity

First and foremost, one needs to consider that the work to be done involves individuals who have been devastated or victimized in some manner. Researchers and their studies are usually sanctioned by an oversight process. Typically, these overseeing bodies are academic institutions, large companies, professional organizations, or philanthropic groups. Although these organizations impose guidelines for research, victims need additional consideration that usually supersedes these standards. With sensitivity and empathy, researchers maybe able to form relationships and assist others while still carrying out research. But victims should never feel like "subjects" of a study. They have already been subjected to multiple losses, including a loss of identity, and should not have their identities compromised any further. The collection of data should not be invasive or impose any additional challenge to the victims or their families. The data collection should revolve around a service or practice that actually enhances the life of the victim. Demographic studies or predisaster data should be collected as part of a relief effort with a distinct goal, not attached solely to a research effort. One way to successfully accomplish this is by continuous note taking while in the field.

A Diary

Oftentimes a piece of paper and a pencil are all that are available during a crisis. A daily journal is an excellent way to preserve what has transpired during the course of a particular event. A daily journal is also an important aid for the process of debriefing, which is discussed in greater detail in later chapters. Many individuals use a journal or diary so that they can share and gain some insights into their own feelings. This is of great value, but a record of events can also be useful for research purposes. Daily writing could include data collected in a systematic way or following a given set of parameters. In this way, over a period of time, one would be able to make statements about the population he or she has served. For example, accounts in my journal from the Balkans included names, ages, circumstances, and length of time that individuals were refugees.

It also contained such data as whether or not families were to-gether and if they had lost loved ones during the war. After 5 days certain parameters were established. Out of the 45 refugees who were interviewed in three different camps, 100% had lost a loved one, 100% had had their homes destroyed, 100% were displaced from their families, 89% had witnessed firsthand a shooting or death, and 82% were involved in a recovery group. Although this appears to be simple demographic information, it can be useful for future work. One could look at the individuals today and see whether those who were involved in recovery activities had better outcomes than individuals who were not.

Resources are often scarce during disaster relief efforts. The technology that we are afforded in our everyday lives is not at hand. A simple diary prepared in advance, with a section for-matted to collect data and to provide space for personal feelings, emotions, and ideas, is a simple but effective tool in collecting valuable data for research.

Collaboration

As previously mentioned, collaboration with others in the field is essential to a relief effort. It is equally important to col-laborate with others when conducting research, in this or any other field of study. Collaboration can be divided into two main categories. The first involves collaborating with others who have worked in this field of study and gaining knowledge from them so that data collection can be directed. Typically, literature searches, direct contact with other researchers, reading, and vis-its to academic institutions or related organizations are the most helpful vehicles. Although the literature is not overflowing with these types of studies, there is much value in a review of what has been done to date. Anyone interested in disaster relief would do well to review the literature, even if research is not the primary goal.

Informal and formal conversations with others who have worked in the field is an excellent way to pick up anecdotal information. Often one can learn about positive interventions, mistakes, and even regrets. For example, an individual once told me that he tried never to be without a small voice recorder of some type that would fit in his pocket and could be used at a moment's notice. I have packed one ever since. This small device can be used to record ideas, data, and conversations that can be reviewed and organized at a later time. Regardless of the means, gaining information from others is useful. The fundamentals of psychological relief are based on interactions, and our learning process in this complex field should be, also.

The second form of collaboration is to work actively with others to achieve a shared goal. As previously stated, the interactions between the lead agency, the disaster relief team, and the local relief team are vital to the success of the psychological relief efforts. These interactions are equally important to any ongoing research effort. Research is facilitated and becomes more relevant when it is valued equally by each of these collaborative groups. Academic, governmental, and charitable institutions usually rely on some ongoing data collection to validate their involvement and continuing efforts. Lead agencies, however, are often not physically situated in a position to carry out the data collection. They must rely on workers in the field to collect data in a meaningful way. It is easy to understand why the disaster relief team and the local relief team have an integral role in this process.

The disaster relief team is often responsible for spawning an idea or initiating the data collection. This group is made up of trained providers who are more likely to have good ideas about what data would be meaningful to others in the field. This disaster relief team is frequently charged with introducing and explaining the significance of the research to the local relief team. The research must be relevant to the local relief team in order for it to embrace the work within the context of a disaster. In addition, the research should provide a vehicle that has immediate significance and utility. Typically, the circumstances of a disaster are not conducive to ideas or a hypothesis that is far-reaching in nature.

Simple studies based on interventions are both easy to conduct and meaningful. In Croatia, during the time when children were being relocated into refugee camps, they were often asked to draw pictures of their homes and families. The initial drawings were gruesome depictions of burning homes, bombs dropping on towns, family members being shot or captured, and related acts of war and aggression. After the children were relocated to the camps and started attending school and play groups, the character of their drawings changed dramatically. They drew pictures of their new homes, children playing, families doing things together, and, probably most significant, flowers on the graves of those lost in the war. A quick glance at the drawings also showed a difference in color choice and life forms included in the pictures. The earlier, somewhat somber, pictures of death and destruction gave way in time to a colorful palette and flowers. The children completed their drawings in art groups which not only reflected their change in attitude but also provided a forum for discussion and a safe arena in which to discuss their feelings with others.

Research is essential to improving our disaster relief efforts. The utility of replicating success is obvious, but research is also a way of demonstrating to others the merits and outcomes of a relief effort. Funding is an essential component of any successful relief effort. And individuals, groups, organizations, and governments are more apt to contribute to a cause that has demonstrated its efficacy. These same sources are also more willing to provide additional dollars to extend efforts when outcomes can be measured and replicated. Research successfully implemented, though typically associated with academicians and higher learning, has implications far beyond classrooms and libraries.

SUMMARY

Psychological relief for victims of disaster or trauma reaches far beyond the scope of traditional therapy and treatment, especially when the victims are children. Dislocated from family, school, and community, children will be hard pressed to understand their new circumstances. The devastation that often accompanies war, natural disasters and violence is not best handled in the privacy of offices. Mental health workers who provide psychological assistance must realize that they have an obligation to treat families and communities, while always keeping in mind the culture and region they find themselves in. Much more can be learned about a victim when one is cognizant of the culture and the socioeconomic circumstances in which he or she lives.

Families and communities are an integral part of children's lives. How a family or community responds to disaster is often reflected in the behavior of children. How a family and community heals is always reflected in the healing of children.

REFERENCES

Adjukovic, D. (1994, July). *Development of comprehensive psychosocial assistance programs for refugees in camps*. Twenty-third International Congress of Applied Psychology, Madrid, Spain.

Adjukovic, D., & Ljuubotina, D. (1995, May). *Traumatic stress in children and adolescents*. Paper presented at the Fourth European Conference on Traumatic Stress, Paris.

Bowlby, J. (1973). *Attachment and loss*. (Vol. 2). New York: Basic Books.

Brown, L. (1986). Stressful life events as perceived by children. *Dissertation Abstracts International* (UMI No. 8578539).

Dzepina, M., Prebeg, Z., Juresa, V., Bogdan-Matjan, K., Brkljaccic, D., Erddelj-Stivicic, B., et al. (1992) Suffering of Croatian school children during war. *Croatian Medical Journal, 33* (War Suppl. 2), 40–44.

Elkind, R., & Weiner, W. (1972). *Child development: A core approach*. New York: Wiley.

Facts for families: Children and firearms. (1992, October). *Journal of the American Academy of Child and Adolescent Psychiatry, 37*.

Galante, R., & Foa, D. (1986). An epidemiological study of psychic trauma and treatment effectiveness after a natural disaster. *Journal of the American Academy of Child Psychiatry, 25*, 357–363.

Garabino, J. (1991). Developmental consequences of living in dangerous and unstable environments: The situation of refugee children. In M. McCallin (Ed.), *The psychological well-being of refugee children, practice and policy issues* (pp. 1–23). Geneva, Switzerland: International Catholic Child Bureau.

Howard, S. J., & Gordon, N. S. (1972). Mental health intervention in a major disaster. San Fernando, CA: Child Guidance Clinic.

Joshi, P. (1996, October). *Children and violence*. Paper presented at the meeting of the Johns Hopkins Children's Center Colloquium on Children and Violence, Baltimore.

Opie, N., Goodwin, T., Finke, L., Lee, B., Beatty, J., & Van Epps, J. (1992). The effect of a bereavement group experience on bereaved children's and adolescents' affective and somatic distress. *Journal of Child and Adolescent Psychiatric Mental Health Nursing, 5* (1), 20–26.

Taylor, C. (1996, October). *Experiences abroad*. Paper presented at the meeting of the Johns Hopkins Children's Center Colloquium on Children and Violence, Baltimore.

Disaster Mental Health

TRAUMA RELIEF, CONCEPTS, AND THEORY

John D. Weaver

People are almost always *changed* by the traumatic events they face during their lives, but they need not be *damaged* by those events.

ANYONE WHO WATCHES TV OR READS NEWSPAPERS REALIZES that potentially traumatic life events are always just a heartbeat away. Everything from a seemingly minor traffic accident to a house fire, a violent crime, or a catastrophic natural or human-caused disaster can, in a matter of minutes, change our lives forever. Helping people cope with the emotional fallout from such traumatic events is the focus of the expanding field of practice that has come to be known as *disaster mental health* (DMH).

Most mental health professionals are extensively trained in the diagnosis and treatment of persons with mental illness. Unfortunately, little time is spent preparing those same professionals for helping people cope with the "normal" stress reactions that commonly result when people are faced with the abnormally stressful conditions that follow disasters (or other life crises).

Helpers need to make a mental shift from an orientation focused on pathology to one focused on wellness. Rather than treatment, most victims (and other helpers) simply need opportunities to vent, with active listening, psychoeducation, and emotional support.

This chapter offers an overview of key DMH principles and techniques, with emphasis on teaching two key concepts—defusing and debriefing. Crisis intervention skills are seldom taught in traditional undergraduate or graduate school settings, and yet they can greatly assist all clinicians, even in our more typical, nondisaster practice settings, when we find ourselves working with clients who have undergone traumatic life experiences. Also, for those readers who may be interested in volunteering some of their time for actual disaster relief work, this chapter provides some basic information about the programs and services offered by the American Red Cross (ARC) DMH Services (DMHS) team.

EARLY BEGINNINGS

Healthcare providers have been struggling with the physical and emotional fallout of traumatic events for centuries. The evolution of modern disaster mental health practices can be traced to World War I, when workers found themselves treating conditions that came to be known as *shell shock, battle fatigue*, and *combat stress*. Those mental health professionals were learning lessons that helped lay the foundation for later relief work following traumatic events and disasters.

DMH may have actually gotten its formal start at one of the

most notorious fires in U.S. history, at the Coconut Grove night-club in Boston in 1943. This horrendous nightclub fire killed 493 people, many of whom were soldiers. Lindemann (1944) wrote of his experience as one of the mental health professionals from nearby Harvard Medical School and Massachusetts General Hospital who helped the survivors deal with their acute grief reactions. He was the first to describe the *disaster syndrome* (or *survivor syndrome*):

> a combination of symptoms victims of disasters commonly display—shock; suggestibility; firmly established memories of the event; possible guilt at having survived; acute stress reactions that might include insomnia, nightmares, memory difficulties, anxiety symptoms, sadness, mood swings, loss of interest in social activities/hobbies/sexual activity; poor work or school performance; and, for many, a need to tell one's disaster stories over and over with surprising detail. (Weaver, 1999, p. 398)

Lindemann (1944) and his colleagues also found that allowing (and encouraging) survivors to express their feelings and begin to grieve resulted in recovery that was faster and more thorough.

BASIC DMH TERMS AND CONCEPTS

The central principle of DMH is that the target population primarily consists of "normal" people (those who were functioning well prior to the trauma) who have now experienced an abnormally stressful life event. Victims generally do not stop functioning, but they do react in fairly predictable ways (with some differences due to age and level of maturity). By using various crisis intervention techniques, outreach services, and psychoeducational approaches, the victims and relief workers can be triaged, briefly counseled or referred for formal services (if needed), and returned to predisaster levels of functioning as quickly as possible. The goal of DMH is to help assure that the *victims* become *survivors* by doing whatever can be done to prevent long-term negative consequences of the psychological trauma, such as the development of a Post Traumatic Stress Disorder (PTSD).

As indicated in the epigraph to this chapter, people will definitely be changed by traumatic life events, but they need not perceive those changes as being irreparable emotional damage. Reflecting on how losses from an unexpected flood had affected her life, one young woman said, "I guess I'm a different person. . . . I matured more than I really wanted to." Most people will never forget the event or how it has changed them. DMH workers strive to help people cope with those changes until they can adjust to their loss(es) and establish a new sense of balance and control in their lives.

Victims who directly experience a disaster or other traumatic event, the *primary level victims*, are generally at greater emotional risk than those who hear about the event, watch it on TV, and so forth, the *secondary level victims* (Bolin, 1985). Victims who actively use *task-oriented*, problem-solving approaches generally respond better and faster and have more positive outcomes than those who have *defense-oriented* reactions (Carson & Butcher, 1992). Thus, those who appraise the damage and losses, begin cleaning up and fill out forms to seek aid or insurance monies will not need as much intervention as those who engage in excessive crying, social isolation, and heavy use of denial and repression (generally expecting things will never get better). For this latter group, the basic psychological concepts of *learned helplessness* and the *self-fulfilling prophecy* often come into play.

Post Traumatic Stress Reactions (PTSR) involve the presentation of an array of PTSD-like symptoms that occur very shortly after a traumatic event but do not last long enough to warrant a diagnosis of PTSD. Signs of PTSR include:

- Recurrent and intrusive thoughts or recollections of the traumatic event
- Recurrent dreams of the trauma
- Believing or feeling as if the traumatic event were recurring
- Avoidance of thoughts, feelings, or conversations associated with the trauma
- Avoidance of activities, places, or people that arouse recollections of the trauma
- Decreased interest or participation in significant activities
- Sleep difficulties
- Irritability, angry outbursts
- Difficulty with concentration

These reactions are quite common among survivors of disaster events (Mays, 1993). The goal of most DMH interventions is to help victims recognize, understand, and accept some of the normal changes that often occur in the days and weeks following any traumatic event, so that these normal reactions need not lead into the development of a full-fledged PTSD.

Although DMH interventions can be useful years after a traumatic event has happened, it is best to offer services as soon as possible after the disaster or traumatic event. Sometimes dubbed the *wet cement theory*, the notion is that processing the mix of thoughts, feelings, and emotions is generally easier while things are fresh in victims' minds, just as it is easier to smooth rough spots in cement before it hardens. Reframing errant perceptions through psychoeducational approaches can best be accomplished before the individual is allowed to negatively embellish what will already be lasting, painful memories. There may even be some nasty rumors that can be dispelled or misconceptions corrected that will make the recovery a bit easier. In home fires, for example, the fatalities usually occur from smoke inhalation, and this often happens even before flames are seen and the fire department is called. Not realizing this, neighbors may be angry at themselves or at the fire department for not preventing the deaths with some quicker action. It provides some measure of relief in this situation to know that nothing more could have been done.

Meichenbaum's (1985) concept of *stress inoculation* is useful in relief work. Provide incoming workers with detailed briefings about the disaster and the nature/culture/diversity of those who have been traumatized. Teach the disaster victims and relief workers how they have been changed by their experience. Tell everyone about how certain sights, sounds, and smells will likely revive some of the painful thoughts and feelings they are now having throughout the rest of their lives. Warn them about holiday stress and anniversary reactions. These lessons will help them survive the difficult times that are to come by demystifying the recovery process and adding more sense of personal control over the expected reactions.

PHASES OF REACTION AND RECOVERY

Disaster literature suggests that persons or communities struck by disaster will generally pass through four distinct phases of response:

- *Heroic phase* (may begin before impact and last up to 1 week afterward). People struggle to prevent loss of lives and reduce property damage.
- *Honeymoon phase* (may last 2 weeks to 2 months). Massive relief efforts lift spirits of survivors and hopes for a quick recovery run high; this optimism is often short-lived.
- *Disillusionment phase* (may last from several months to 1 year or more). Sometimes called the *second disaster*, when the realities of bureaucratic paperwork set in, and recovery is delayed; outside help leaves and people realize they must do more themselves.
- *Reconstruction phase* (may take several years). Normal functioning is gradually reestablished. (Weaver, 1995, pp. 31–32)

During the heroic phase, energy levels are high, and emotions are very strong. Altruism is a common response. Disasters tend to bring out the best and, sadly, the worst human behavior. People who have lost control of their lives will feel more like victims than survivors will. Neighbors help neighbors as people pitch in and do whatever it takes to assist others who are struggling to survive. Energy is channeled into efforts to save lives and property. Police, fire/rescue, and emergency relief teams (e.g., ARC, Salvation Army, and other relief groups) offer immediate help. So do families, friends, neighbors, schools, churches, and employers.

In the honeymoon phase victims realize they have shared and survived the disaster. Public and private relief services appear to be capable of quickly getting things back to normal. There is a strong sense of community. Lots of focused activities continue to channel energy (e.g., assessing losses, cleaning up, and beginning repairs). For some, the mourning process slowly begins. Families, friends, neighbors, schools, churches, Federal Emergency Management Agency (FEMA) personnel, relief workers, employers, local human service agencies, and many other community groups are willing to meet specific needs of those affected by the trauma.

Disillusionment begins as soon as the typical, long-term challenges of recovery begin to surface (e.g., working with relief agencies, insurance companies, FEMA, and other government bureaucracies). Some call this the *second disaster*, and it can last for years. Anger, frustration, sadness, fear, resentment, and a further sense of victimization are common feelings. The unrealized hopes for a full and speedy recovery are dashed by the realities of how painfully slow the process will be. The strong sense of community is now gone. People give up on the notion that others can help them and begin to focus on doing things for themselves. The large relief organizations are scaling down their operations or pulling out. Local help is strained and dwindling. Family and friends seem to be less helpful and supportive.

Reconstruction begins once people are ready to let go of the anger of the previous phase and move on with their lives. For most people, there is acceptance of how long and how difficult the recovery process can be. But, for some, there may be continuing turmoil and possibly the development of a PTSD. The survivors have retaken control of their lives and of responsibility for their own recovery. They can see progress, work toward their goals, and accept the pace of rebuilding. Family members, friends, churches, a few agencies, and community groups (plus local branches of large, national relief agencies) often remain active throughout the whole ordeal.

FEELINGS AND COMMON REACTIONS

These are the common feelings and reactions that most victims will express or display in the wake of traumatic events:

- Basic survival concerns
- Grief over loss of loved ones or prized possessions
- Separation anxiety and fears for safety of significant others
- Regressive behaviors such as thumb sucking and bed-wetting in children
- Relocation and isolation fears
- A need to express thoughts and feelings about having experienced the disaster
- A need to feel one is a part of the community and its rebuilding efforts
- Altruism and the desire to help others cope and rebuild their homes and their lives (Farberow, 1978; Weaver, 1995)

The next two sections provide a very brief overview of some specific age-related reactions to trauma.

Children and Adolescents

The American Academy of Pediatrics Work Group on Disasters (Center for Mental Health Service, 1995) notes that disasters often cause behavioral changes and regression in children. Many react with fear and show clear signs of anxiety about recurrence of the disaster event(s). Sleep disturbances are very common among children (and adults) and can best be addressed by quickly returning to (or establishing) a familiar bedtime routine. Inability to do this proved to be a major problem following the earthquake in Northridge, California, as frequent aftershocks and displacement from homes made it difficult for anyone to return to regular sleep routines. Many families were also all sleeping together in the same bed long after the main quake.

Friedman et al. (1995) and Weaver (1995) also note that school avoidance may lead to the development of school phobias if children are not quickly returned to their normal routine of school attendance. In some disasters the schools themselves may be damaged and inoperable. This, and the need to be bussed to other, unfamiliar buildings, further add to the stresses on children. The Northridge earthquake and its aftershocks resulted in many children staying home for weeks, fearful to leave their parents' sides for the length of the school day.

In terms of psychological losses, children and teens often experience a loss of innocence. For many, their whole world may seem less safe and less secure than it was prior to the traumatic event. It tends to make them face tough issues like death and bereavement sooner than the adults in their lives had hoped would happen. Remember the quote from the young woman mentioned earlier, "I guess I'm a different person. . . . I matured more than I really wanted to." After making that comment she smiled and giggled, but the serious look in her eyes clearly showed her continuing efforts to grapple with the new reality.

Adults

Friedman et al. (1995) and Weaver (1995) found that adults often report mild symptoms of depression and anxiety. They can feel haunted by visual memories of the event. They may experience psychosomatic illnesses. Preexisting physical problems, such as heart trouble, diabetes, and ulcers, may worsen in response to the increased level of stress. They may show anger, mood swings, suspicion, irritability, or apathy. Changes in appetite and sleep patterns are quite common. Adults, too, may have a period of poor performance at work or school and they may undergo some social withdrawal.

Middle-aged adults, in particular, may experience additional stress, if they lose the security of their planned (and possibly paid-for) retirement home (or financial nest egg) or if they are forced to pay for extensive rebuilding. Older adults will greatly miss their daily routines and will suffer strong feelings of loss from missing friends and loved ones. They may also suffer feelings of significant loss from the absence of their home or apartment or its sentimental objects (especially items such as paintings, antiques, family Bibles, photo albums, and films or videotapes), which tied them to their past.

Adults living in group residential rehabilitation settings (mental health, mental retardation, and substance abuse facilities) and institutions (prisons, hospitals, boarding homes, and nursing facilities) may react in the same ways in which others in the community react to the disaster. For these groups there is often an overriding sense of isolation and dependence, which they may have felt before the disaster. These negative feelings can worsen during the recovery period, when family members and friends are lost as casualties of the event or as captives of the cleanup effort. Either way, the persons in these residential settings generally receive less social contact and will tend to feel more forgotten and alone.

Timing of the onset of these changes varies with each person, as does duration. Some symptoms occur immediately, whereas others may not show until weeks later. Just about all of these things are considered normal reactions, as long as they do not last more than several weeks to a few months.

KEY DMH GUIDELINES

Myers (1994) and Weaver (1995) offer several critically important concepts for DMH workers to keep in mind. The first is to
avoid using mental health labels and jargon. People who are
having typical stress reactions may already be fearful that they
may be losing their sanity. Anything that reinforces fears of potential mental illness can be detrimental. DMH workers must
reinforce wellness concepts and downplay illness models.

Most people do not disintegrate. Victims and relief workers
will generally carry on the activities of recovery (cleaning up,
filling out insurance forms, applying for disaster aid, etc.) in
ways that will often surprise newly recruited relief volunteers.
Adrenaline helps make this possible. Eventually, though, victims
and relief workers slow down and begin to take stock of their
situations. It is during those periods of reflection on losses and
unexpected change that DMH education and support can be of
greatest help.

Victims (and relief workers) respond to DMH workers who
show active interest and concern. Those who have experienced
disasters or traumatic events need to tell their stories, and they
welcome relief workers' full attention, advice, and support.
Many times, workers will find that victims will retell their stories
several times, needing to externalize the painful memories and
to seek validation and support from others.

Workers need to abandon traditional office-based approaches. Given the stigma of mental illness, those who might
benefit the most from DMH interventions are often fearful of
seeking help. To be successful, DMH services must be offered
on an outreach basis. This is done by getting the relief workers
out into the community gathering spots and getting the educa-

tional messages into the area's popular print and broadcast media.

Be sensitive to cultural, ethnic, racial, and socioeconomic diversity. Things that mental health professionals may take for granted in their usual practice, such as eye contact and personal distance (personal space), vary greatly among different cultures. Similarly, we all differ in how we experience and mourn losses in our lives. Some openly express feelings, whereas others are less apt to share emotional experiences with strangers. Relief workers need to be extremely sensitive to diversity issues. The pool of relief workers should reflect a similar mix of sex, race, and culture to those in the population that they are serving.

The disaster climate has a way of generating lots of rumors. One town experienced heavy rains, and two elderly persons died in the flash flooding that resulted. Word quickly spread of the deaths, and, within a few days, the rumor was spreading among the kids in the local school system that two little children had died. People tend to crave sensational information and often put an exaggeratedly negative slant on things when facts are not available. DMH workers must often dispel misinformation while doing DMH interventions. In the case of this school system, they had to offer children the facts that it had actually been two elderly victims who died—and also to openly discuss the children's fears that they might have died.

Disasters bring out the best and the worst in people. Several summers ago there was a large apartment fire in Philadelphia that caught national media attention. Neighbors had rushed to help get victims out of the burning structure. Meanwhile, other neighbors looted the helping neighbors' homes. Whenever a hurricane hits a coastal town, hundreds of volunteers from groups such as the Salvation Army and the ARC put their own lives on hold and rush to offer help. At the same time, dishonest roofers enter the area, offer repairs, take money to purchase supplies, then disappear without doing the work. Others may overcharge for bags of ice or similar necessities. This mix of best and worst can be very demoralizing to both victims and relief workers.

Helpers are subject to a vast array of physical and emotional responses to crises, including burnout. Figley (1995) notes, "there is a cost to caring" (p. 1). Hearing the stories of personal trauma over and over again often takes a toll on the relief workers. At the same time, the workers are usually separated from their own families and other support systems. Sometimes helpers reach a point at which they have no more to give, finding themselves burning out. They too are now victims in need of care and support. The resulting condition has been dubbed compassion fatigue, secondary traumatic stress disorder, covictimization, and vicarious traumatization. Care must be taken to practice self-care, to limit further exposure, and to routinely process strong reactions through the use of journaling, DMH peer support, defusing, and debriefing (discussed in a subsequent section).

Workers can find strength (and peer supports) in numbers. Myers (1994) and Weaver (1995) stress the importance of utilizing a team approach when organizing disaster relief programs. The availability of a team eases the stress on individual workers by allowing an equitable division of labor and responsibilities. Use of a team also encourages development of natural support systems among those doing the interventions. Once the work is completed, the team members debrief one another about shared experiences. DMH workers generally report positive outcomes from this shared intervention process.

One DMH experience may be enough to get you "hooked"

(or to help you determine that this is not something you would ever want to do again). As strange as this may seem to those who have not experienced it, relief work is highly addictive for many volunteers, regardless of their relief functions or roles. For DMH workers, the practice experiences are wonderfully rich and professionally rewarding. In fact, among many of my friends who have become DMH workers, relief work has rekindled the kind of helping spirit that they have not felt since shortly after graduate school.

Some describe their first experience as "a calling" to their DMH volunteer career, similar to the ways clergy report being called into their ministry. Others who volunteer will find that the work is too stressful or emotionally demanding. DMH work often involves long hours of intensive debriefing, education, and support concerning issues of bereavement and loss, done in working conditions that can be oppressive. Volunteers who have negative first experiences generally do not seek future assignments.

TRIAGE

Traumatic events vary greatly in scope. Whenever more than one person has been affected by the trauma, there is a need for mental health screening and the setting of priorities, just as there is with physical injuries. Helpers need to establish a presence in the relief site areas that will be frequented by the victims. They also need to visit the injured and make condolence calls to those who have lost loved ones.

Much DMH work is done while "hanging out" with victims and other relief workers. Most interventions are very brief contacts, many being 15 minutes or less in length. Those persons who are having more serious difficulties need more careful attention and longer, more formal interviews. The following questions should help clarify some types of information that must be gathered while screening persons with more significant negative reactions (Weaver, 1995, pp. 86–89):

- What drew special attention to this person? What are the person's presenting problems? How long have the problems existed? What help (support, education, or treatment services) has the person received and from whom?
- What prescription and nonprescription (over-the-counter) medications are being used by the person for physical problems? What psychotropic medication, if any, is the person taking for any psychiatric condition(s) for which he or she is receiving treatment? Is the person self-medicating (abusing street drugs, prescription or nonprescription medications, or alcohol)?
- Has the person had a recent physical examination to rule out any physical problems that might be causing (or adding to) the current problems? Is there a family history of mental illness? What changes in mood, behavior, sleep, appetite, ability to concentrate, or motivation are present?
- If depression is mentioned (or seems obvious), ask about current (and previous) suicidal thoughts and attempts. If anger or poor impulse control are issues, explore thoughts (and history of actions) involving harm to others. If the person is hearing voices, displays suspiciousness of others, sees things, feels odd sensations, believes he or she is being controlled by others (or the media), and so forth, these are often good indicators of serious mental illness.
- It is always a good idea to conclude any screening interview with a general, open-ended question that allows the indi-

vidual to fill in any gaps (Weaver, 1995). Say something like, "Is there anything I did not ask you that might be important for me to know about how things are going with you since the disaster?" Keep the possibility of abusive behavior in mind. Physical or psychological child abuse, spouse abuse, elder abuse, and other abusive relationships may worsen under the stress. Substance abuse also tends to rise, adding to tensions and further fueling physical or psychological abuse issues.

DMH INTERVENTIONS

Weaver (1995) offers several practical tips on how to offer DMH intervention. First, DMH workers need to get people talking, keep people busy, and begin problem solving. Much of the content of DMH conversations will involve themes of loss and bereavement. People will be attempting to come to grips with the mixed feelings they are having about lost family treasures (photo albums, Bibles, dishes, furniture, or possibly their entire home), pets, friends, and loved ones. They will also be questioning why this had to occur and, at the same time, struggling to find some meaning in what has happened. They will be hopeful that emotional relief and some sort of closure will come soon.

Unfortunately, anecdotal evidence that I have gained from interviews with victims and other relief workers indicates that the process of mourning the losses and reordering one's life after a major disaster often takes 2 to 7 years, much as it does whenever someone close to you dies. Informing people about this possible time line and warning them about the rough road ahead is often very helpful. Although it may seem that this could further devastate them, they actually find it empowering to know that they will gradually get better and that they will likely become stronger throughout this healing process.

DMH contacts can be made at work locations such as disaster sites, staging areas, shelters, feeding locations, service centers, and so on. Helpers need to "work the crowds" at relief points, visit remote sites, do home visits, and make condolence calls. Outreach services and public education are essential because only a small number of those persons emotionally touched by a disaster may seek direct-care services. Workers need to utilize print and broadcast media to broadly distribute timely information about the normal reactions people experience during the recovery (a period far longer than most people realize). Several excellent brochures are available through ARC and FEMA, with many also printed in Spanish, to help spread critical messages.

The following pointers should also be kept in mind (Weaver, 1995):

- Be patient.
- Listen to what everyone has to say and encourage family members, friends, coworkers, and so forth to also do this with one another.
- Show active interest, concern, and acceptance, and model this behavior for others.
- Allow time for telling and retelling of the stories that have grown out of the disaster events, including the ghastly details you would rather avoid. Adults and many children will do this verbally, but adults should also expect to see children and teenagers expressing their reactions to the traumatic event(s) in their play, their artwork, and their writings. Do not be surprised, for instance, if you see a child's

dollhouse getting washed away, shaken, or blown apart several times each day following a flood, a quake, or a tornado.

- Give simple, brief, honest answers to questions about what is to come and help people focus on immediate problem solving. Encourage parents to do this with their children and teachers to do this with their students.
- Try to shift the focus from individuals who are struggling with their own individual problems to families or groups who are tackling shared issues (challenges). Things will seem less overwhelming when there is a team of people working toward solutions.
- Help people see the importance of reestablishing predisaster routines (eating meals together, attending school and work, having a set bedtime, etc.) and rituals. These little things often can make a big difference, helping the environment seem more like it was before the disaster struck.
- Allow for special needs and offer a little bit of extra attention to those who are at risk. Help parents understand that children who have slipped back into bed-wetting, for instance, are having a typical reaction to the stress of the event. The kids are not any happier about these little developmental glitches than their parents are. With some support, they will soon get back on track.
- Be honest about your own feelings, fears, and reactions to the traumatic event and encourage victims to do the same thing. If people are mourning losses, they should do so openly and share the experience with others. Modeling grief and bereavement practices for children is especially important for those who may have never experienced the death of someone close to them. All children need to see is that the surviving adults cared deeply for those who were lost.

- Above all, encourage the use of the resources at hand in people's natural support groups. Family members (immediate and extended), peers, staff members at school or work, and members of church groups are often the best sources of support. There are also many others, such as fellow members of sports teams, scouting organizations, fraternities and sororities, workout places, and so on.
- Any place people gather and talk should be considered a potential spot for providing information and support, even restaurants (especially popular diners), barber shops, hair salons, and malls. A part of the message everyone is given must be:

WHENEVER YOU HAVE QUESTIONS OR IF THINGS ARE NOT GRADUALLY IMPROVING, PLEASE SEEK PROFESSIONAL HELP.

DEFUSING AND DEBRIEFING

Defusing and debriefing are the two most significant forms of DMH intervention. Both allow trauma victims and relief workers opportunities to ventilate about their traumatic memories, the resulting stresses, the losses, and methods of coping. Either process helps encourage people to begin talking things out within the security of a safe and supportive atmosphere (Weaver, 1995). Both provide some needed structure to the helping interviews, and either can be done with individuals or groups.

Defusing

Defusing, as the name implies, is not unlike the process of taking a fuse out of a bomb (or an explosive situation) and intervening to stop something before it becomes worse. The defusing process usually involves informal and impromptu sessions. A DMH worker might witness an emotional interchange between a victim and another staff member and, soon afterward, approach one or both of them to open a dialogue. This, in turn, helps the workers release thoughts and feelings that might not otherwise be appropriately expressed. Suppression or repression of this kind of highly charged material can lead to troubled relationships and development of any number of stress-related physical or mental illnesses.

Here are some ways in which defusing can be integrated into everyday activities:

- Greeting a victim who is waiting in line at a disaster service center and offering a snack or a drink
- Playing a game with a child in an emergency shelter
- Making a purchase from a clerk at a store in the disaster area
- Ordering a meal while in the field
- Running into a co-worker at the copy machine
- Going out to eat with other staff members

What do these situations have in common? Each offers an opportunity to begin a healing process for someone who is anxious to tell his or her story. Sometimes all that is needed is a little eye contact and the stories will begin to pour out. Sound too easy? Just think of how many times you have managed to get people's life histories (or detailed injustices) while you are waiting in the checkout line at the grocery store—unsolicited information, but you got it anyway.

Although informal and immediate, the defusing often becomes a mini-debriefing and can follow one of the formats discussed in the next section. Because the allotted time is generally too brief, it is simply a starting point. Further intervention may be needed, and this can be anything from offering ongoing support (e.g., briefly touching base with the persons or groups in the coming days and weeks) to scheduling and providing formal debriefing sessions.

Debriefing

Debriefings are formal meetings that can be handled individually or in small groups. They are generally held shortly after an unusually stressful incident has ended, strictly for dealing with the emotional residuals of the event. Any location that is large enough to hold the group and that can be secured to assure privacy is appropriate for use. Sessions may require blocks of time that are several hours in length, particularly if a process such as Mitchell's (1983) *Critical Incident Stress Debriefing* (CISD) model is used.

Whenever possible, everyone involved in the event should attend the debriefing(s). Many organizations recommend (or require) attending defusing and debriefing sessions whenever certain types of incidents occur. ARC, for instance, offers defusing as necessary, throughout each person's tour of duty at a disaster scene. ARC also recommends (but does not require) having a debriefing before workers leave for home. Once ARC workers get home, their local ARC chapter usually offers them a formal debriefing.

At the morgue following the 1994 crash of Flight 427 near Pittsburgh, volunteer *trackers* and *scribes* (persons who escorted the remains of the 132 victims through the identification process) were offered graphic prebriefings, a form of stress inoculation. They were required to attend debriefings at the end of their shifts. Even those attendees who initially resented being required to attend quickly found themselves getting actively involved in the process. We began the debriefings by warning them about two little things that happened that might have forever changed lasting memories of two common objects—ordinary cafeteria trays, which were used to carry body parts, and Vicks VapoRub, which was used in masks to offset other unpleasant odors. Once they heard these two clear and simple examples of the information and support we were offering, things opened up and sharing began. Many expressed their gratitude, and all seemed to value the opportunity to be debriefed (Weaver, 1995).

The CISD process (Mitchell, 1983) was designed to help *first responders* (police officers, firefighters, emergency medical technicians, etc.), overcome the emotional aftereffects of *critical incidents* (e.g., line-of-duty deaths). Mitchell was well aware of how often the witnessing of deaths by fire, line-of-duty shootings, street violence, motor vehicle accidents, and other traumatic events was taking its toll on these emergency workers, sometimes even causing them to suddenly walk away from their chosen careers rather than face the next incident. He designed the method to help workers quickly begin to process their thoughts and feelings about the traumatic events. Done well, it helps keep good people physically and emotionally healthy, and it also helps keep them on the job.

Sessions conducted under the Mitchell model are usually held within the first 24 to 72 hours after the traumatic event, with follow-up sessions as needed. Given the nature of disasters, many of the victims are not available for a formal meeting that quickly. Fortunately, the debriefing process is still beneficial, even when the sessions are held long after the event. In fact, the best time for many debriefing sessions is about 1 week after any funerals have been held. Funerals allow some closure to the traumatic event, thus setting up the proper climate for this type of reflection on the event and for looking ahead to how lives will be changed by it.

There are now several debriefing models (McCammon & Allison, 1995). The ARC DMHS team uses the *Multiple Stressor Debriefing* model (Armstrong, Lund, McWright, & Tichenor, 1995). Although the various models differ in number and type of phases (or stages), they all address the same basic elements that Mitchell's original process sought to examine. Each model helps people cope with the sights, sounds, smells, thoughts, feelings, symptoms, and memories that are part of a normal stress reaction to a traumatic event.

Whatever model is used, allow adequate time for people to ventilate, especially during the initial phases or stages of the process, when facts, thoughts, and feelings are being discussed. Encourage detailed expression of the most vivid or graphic negative images and memories. Think of it as cleaning out an emotional wound before allowing it to heal with foreign material still on the inside. Improper procedure with a bad cut promotes infection. Improper procedure here means that the emotional wounds can be too easily reopened by future stressful events, increasing the possibility of developing PTSD.

Although the focus of this chapter is on large-scale disaster events, DMH techniques work equally well in day-to-day practice situations. Local, single-family fires and other small-scale disasters often cause the same traumatic responses as do the larger scale events, and victims of both respond well to these interventions. Most mental health professionals who have not been taught about defusing or debriefing report being amazed at how helpful these simple but powerful tools can then become in their day-to-day practices for helping clients cope with various life crises.

Clients who have experienced the loss of a loved one, crime victimization, or any traumatic events can be helped with this approach. Defusing and debriefing can also help prevent burn-out when used to support co-workers who find themselves in highly stressful situations. Normalize their experiences. Teach them about stress reactions. Provide stress inoculation about anniversary reactions and other issues they will eventually face. Offer support and try to anchor a positive image and outlook for their successful recovery. End by thanking them for coming and taking part in the debriefing process; shake their hands or give a hug as each person leaves the session.

Everly (1995) cites 10 factors that seem to contribute to the effectiveness of the debriefing process. To summarize his points, debriefing involves the use of a highly structured, cognitive-behavioral discussion of the trauma. It is generally provided as an early intervention. Sessions are frequently done in group settings, conveying hope and caring in a manner that will garner lasting peer support. Also, and central to all of the other factors, is the finding by Pennebaker and Sussman (1988) that structured cathartic ventilation of traumatic experiences is highly related to subsequent reductions in stress arousal (Everly, 1995).

Guidelines for Organizing Community Debriefings

In addition to the many ARC DMHS teams located throughout the country, county and state mental health office DMH teams, regional CISD or CISM (critical incident stress management) teams, and fully trained teams from other agencies may all be available to help when mutual aid is needed. It is always best to affiliate with an established team and practice within existing boundaries. Trying to independently insert yourself into a working relief operation will only add to the challenges facing those who are managing the relief operation.

The following list is intended to help DMH workers facilitate formal community debriefing sessions, which are often held in the days and weeks following a disaster event.

- Try to find a site that allows separate breakout rooms, so that a large group can be divided into smaller ones. Churches, schools, and other similar buildings are good meeting places.
- When working with several groups, try to locate a neutral spot in the building to which the group that finishes first can go to await the arrival of the other group(s). This same spot is a good place to use for offering simple snacks and drinks, before and after the session.
- Try to get someone from the group of persons who have requested the debriefing to help with preparations by having that person invite the appropriate participants and select the logical meeting place. This screening will help assure confidentiality.
- As the invitations are being made, try to estimate how many persons may attend and how many small groups may be needed. A good rule of thumb is to try to have no more than 12 persons in each small group and to have two facilitators per group.
- To maintain confidentiality and eliminate interruptions, it is helpful to take along an extra person to watch the door. This person can stop anyone who is late (or uninvited) from disrupting the process, and he or she can also intervene with anyone who becomes upset and tries to leave early. In either instance, the extra DMH worker will simply do a one-on-

one intervention (probably a defusing session) and steer the
person in the right direction.

- Take along some appropriate educational handouts. Possi-
  bilities for disasters include these, most of which are ARC
  publications:
  - *After the Fire* (ARC 2207)
  - *After the Flood* (ARC 2204)
  - *After the Quake* (ARC 2201)
  - *After the Storm* (ARC 2206)
  - *After the Tornado* (ARC 2205)
  - *Coping With Disaster, Emotional Health Issues for Vic-
    tims* (ARC 4475)
  - *Helping Children Cope With Disaster* (ARC 4499)
  - Debriefing session handout (a one-page information sheet
    designed to be given to each participant at the start of the
    session; a copy can be found in Table 2.1 at the end of
    this chapter)
- When entering a large room and taking seats, people will
  often form logical subgroups. Use this phenomenon to your
  advantage to help in allocating space and assigning participants and facilitators to the smaller working groups.
- It is important to separate participants into groups by
  trauma-exposure level. If some individuals had low levels
  of exposure to the nastiest sights, sounds, smells, and so
  forth, you will need to avoid exposing them to that new
  stress via the debriefing session. In addition to grouping by
  exposure level, always debrief victims and workers in separate groups, and debrief workers and supervisory personnel in separate groups. This can all be done by simply stat-
  ing to the larger group the intention to divide into smaller
  groups by exposure level, victims or workers, line workers

or supervisors, and so forth, and letting participants then group themselves.

- Facilitators should try to sit on opposite sides of the small group's circle to allow the maximum ability to monitor group dynamics and each other.
- Although participants are not required to speak, it is generally a good idea to try to draw everyone into the conversation and to do so as quickly as possible. Try to have people begin by going around in a circle with introductions. Then, go around again for each person to respond to the fact phase and the feeling phase (or whatever phases are appropriate for the format you are using). After a few times around, a more natural, free-flowing process can be allowed to take place. By structuring it in this way, shy people are more likely to participate and persons with overbearing personalities are less likely to try to take over the session.

Table 2.1 (p. 71) is a sample handout, based on the original Mitchell (1983) CISD model, which I use to help conduct community debriefing sessions. It can serve as a road map for the meeting, helping to guide the participants and the facilitators (some of whom may be first-timers, new to the process) through the session. A similar handout can be developed from any of the debriefing models. Use of this kind of handout helps demystify the process and instills an adult-learning atmosphere for those who might otherwise be somewhat apprehensive.

CASE EXAMPLES

Suicides are often traumatic events for the individuals who are unfortunate enough to discover the bodies. Such was the case in these two situations:

Case 1

An intensive-case manager (a worker with a small caseload of persons with serious mental health conditions) went to one of her client's homes to accompany her to a routine medical appointment. The client did not answer her door, despite the fact that the appointment had been confirmed the previous afternoon. While heading around the back to see if she was there, the worker looked in the window and saw her on her bed. When the landlord and police arrived, the worker's worst fears were realized: the woman had killed herself by overdose. Now the case manager had to face a long day, first with police and the coroner, and then with the client's surviving family members. This was the first time she'd lost a person she'd been helping.

Case 2

A group-home worker was preparing dinner with some of the 10 seriously mentally ill residents she helped supervise. Once the meal was ready, she began calling the others to the table. One did not respond, and when she went to his room, she found him asphyxiated with a plastic bag tied over his head. The death was reported, and, for the next several hours, she worked with the other residents and staff members as all tried to recover from the shocking loss. This was also her first experience with a suicide.

Case Discussion

In both instances the young women who discovered the persons who had committed suicide were very new to the mental health field. Both needed, received, and benefited from immediate defusing interviews. In fact, the defusing sessions, with opportunities to vent and receive emotional support, helped both people get through that first day. Getting through their subsequent days was aided greatly by formal debriefings and peer support.

In Case 1, the defusing and the debriefing were one-on-one situations. In Case 2, things were quite a bit more complicated. The worker who found the deceased person did receive one-on-one defusing and debriefing, but several other levels of intervention were also needed. First, the other nine residents in the home were secondary victims. They had not seen the man as she had, but they still experienced the trauma, and they, too, needed immediate defusing. So did many of the other group-home staff members and the company's management personnel, even those members who were not all on duty that day.

Separate debriefing sessions were held for the residents, the line staff members, and the administrative staff members 4 days after the death. The delay in doing the debriefing sessions was intentional. If they were done too soon, people might still have been in somewhat of a state of shock and disbelief.

The focus in the debriefings tended to vary. The resident debriefings focused on how much the deceased man had always tended to isolate himself from others. This helped them realize that, were they ever feeling that low, they would probably reach out for help and support rather than take their own lives. In the staff session the focus was on the general theme of loss. Many people had recently left the home, some due to "graduation" to a more independent lifestyle and some back into long-term inpatient care, and now a resident had died. The managers were focused on losses they had experienced throughout their careers, some natural and some to suicides; such debriefings tend to foster recollection of painful memories of all similar traumatic life events the participants have experienced.

For the two young women, the debriefings explored several predictable topic areas—the immediate sights, sounds, and smells; the pressure of needing to stay in their professional roles and continuing to do what needed to be done; fear of blame; some questioning as to whether they'd missed an important clue; and questioning why this had happened to them. The first woman was in her first job after graduation from college. She found that intensive-case management was too stressful for her, and she left her position a few months later. The second woman was taking a semester off from college and working to earn tuition money when this happened. At the end of that summer she returned to school to continue studying social work, having learned a lot more about life and about her sense of self as well.

DISASTER RELIEF PROGRAMS

The American Red Cross has been chartered by the U.S. Congress to provide disaster relief services, and they are the best group to call for initial advice about seeking or providing disaster and emergency assistance. ARC has been providing relief services since 1881, and, since 1989, it has taken the lead in recruiting and training volunteers to serve on DMHS teams whenever and wherever their services may be needed (Morgan, 1995).

The American Psychological Association, the American Counseling Association, the National Association of Social Workers, the American Psychiatric Association, the American Association of Marriage and Family Therapists, several professional nursing organizations, and many other such groups have signed letters of agreement with ARC to help support these efforts. Further discussion of the ARC DMHS team's ongoing development and recent experiences in major disasters can be found in Dingman (1995), Armstrong, Lund, McWright, and Tichenor (1995), Weaver (1995, 1996a, 1996b, 1999), and Jacobs, Quevillon, and Ofman (1998).

Anyone who is looking for an experience that will provide new professional challenges may want to consider joining the ARC DMHS team. Once you have qualified and completed training (that is often free and may offer continuing education units), you will be able to travel to disaster relief sites, work with victims (and other relief workers) whose lives have been struck by disasters, and help them, with ARC covering all disaster-related expenses. Participants in ARC training will learn all about the DMHS program's requirements and opportunities to serve, locally and nationally.

In order to qualify for national ARC service, volunteers must also be licensed or certified social workers, psychologists, counselors, family therapists, nurses, or psychiatrists. Persons who are not yet licensed or certified can sometimes serve locally. The rules are rather complicated, and direct supervision by a fully qualified DMHS worker may be required, so check with ARC officials in your area. If you do not qualify for the DMHS function, another popular option is to serve in another ARC specialty, such as family service (a casework function), mass care (for feeding and sheltering), health services, and damage assessment, among many others.

In times of disaster, many local, state, and federal government officials and agencies work closely with ARC and many other volunteer agencies active in disaster (VOAD). Here is a partial list of those VOAD groups that, in addition to ARC, can provide various forms of relief in times of need: Adventist Community Services; American Radio Relay League, Inc.; Ananda Marga Universal Relief Team; Catholic Charities USA; Christian

Disaster Response, A.E.C.C.G.C.; Christian Reformed World Relief Committee; Church of the Brethren; Church World Service; the Episcopal Church; Friends Disaster Service; Inter-Lutheran Disaster Response; Mennonite Disaster Service; Presbyterian Church USA; REACT International, Inc.; the Salvation Army; Society of St. Vincent de Paul; Southern Baptist Convention; United Methodist Church Committee on Relief; and Volunteers of America. There are also several human service programs that offer help as a result of the Stafford Disaster Relief and Emergency Assistance Act and other state and federal legislation and regulations.

Recognizing the quality of the work done by the ARC DMHS program, and acting under the mandate of the Aviation Disaster Family Assistance Act of 1996, the National Transportation Safety Board (NTSB) has designated ARC the independent nonprofit organization with experience in disasters and posttrauma communications with families. The ARC Aviation Incident Response (AIR) team provides assistance to families and to other personnel involved in relief operations following aviation accidents (Jacobs, Quevillon, & Ofman, 1998). Part of the comprehensive approach ARC has taken with the AIR team has been the inclusion of spiritual care and even child-care capacity. The NTSB designation is further evidence that ARC is often the best point of entry and sanction for persons wishing to offer DMH relief services in the aftermath of natural and human-caused disasters.

RELIEF WORKER STRESS

In major disasters, working conditions are sometimes poor, and hours are usually long. Relief workers often put in 12- to 14-hour days and sometimes do so for weeks at a time. DMH team members and other volunteers need to be mindful of stress management and self-care. Burnout is a serious hazard for disaster workers and for everyone doing trauma counseling.

Use of peer support is one of the best methods that can be used to cope with the stresses—make friends and watch out for each other. Appropriate use of breaks, scheduled time off, humor, maintenance of proper diet, exercise, and getting proper amounts of restful sleep are other critical elements in each worker's plan of care. Keeping a personal journal (a log of what was seen, heard, thought, and felt), and writing a narrative at the end of the assignment can be of help, too.

Once a disaster operation (or a stressful crisis counseling session) ends, workers need to make the transition back to their predisaster lives and responsibilities. This can be a challenging time for the worker, his or her family, and those with whom he or she works. It is often wise to try to schedule some time off before returning to normal duties. Workers and volunteers need a defusing and debriefing session once their relief roles end. Disaster service often changes relief workers in a variety of ways, just as it changes the victims.

SUMMARY AND IMPLICATIONS

Disaster relief work and trauma counseling are not for everyone. The physical and emotional challenges of this sort of work test each person in ways that are not always obvious at the outset. Exposure to secondary traumatic stress is a constant risk, and, like second-hand smoke to nonsmokers, there is no good way to assess the risk until the damage has been done. Consequently, workers need to foster peer support, limit their exposure, recognize their own strengths, understand their personal needs, and admit their limitations.

It is a sad fact of life that traumatic events can occur at any time, and major disasters seem to occur somewhere in this country each year. Although the DMH principles presented here can easily be applied to day-to-day crisis counseling situations, it is my hope that some readers may be moved to give some of their time and talents by also becoming disaster relief volunteers.

This chapter is modified from J. D. Weaver, "How to Assist in the Aftermath of Disasters and Other Life Crises," *Innovations in Clinical Practice: A Source Book* (Vol. 17), L. VandeCreek & T. L. Jackson (Eds.), Sarasota, FL: Professional Resource Press. Copyright © 1999 by the Professional Resource Exchange, Inc., P.O. Box 15560, Sarasota, FL 34277-1560. Reprinted by permission.

REFERENCES

Armstrong, K. R., Lund, P. E., McWright, L. T., & Tichenor, V. (1995, January). Multiple stressor debriefing and the American Red Cross: The East Bay fire experience. *Social Work, 40*, 83–90.

Bolin, R. (1985). Disaster characteristics and psychosocial impacts. In B. J. Sowder (Ed.), *Disasters and mental health: Selected contemporary perspectives* (DHHS Publication No. ADM 85-1421, pp. 3–28). Rockville, MD: Center for Mental Health Services.

Carson, R. C., & Butcher, J. N. (1992). *Abnormal psychology and modern life* (9th ed.). New York: HarperCollins.

Dingman, R. (Ed.). (1995, July). Disasters and crises: A mental health counseling perspective [Special issue]. *Journal of Mental Health Counseling 17* (3).

Everly, G. S., Jr. (1995, July). The role of the Critical Incident Stress Debriefing (CISD) process in disaster counseling. *Journal of Mental Health Counseling 17* (3), 278–290.

Farberow, N. L., & Gordon, N. S. (1981). *Manual for child health workers in major disasters.* (DHHS Publication No. ADM 81-1070). Rockville, MD: Center for Mental Health Services.

Figley, C. R. (Ed.). (1995). *Compassion fatigue: Coping with secondary traumatic stress disorder in those who treat the traumatized.* New York: Brunner/Mazel.

Center for Mental Health Services (1995). *Psychosocial issues for children and families in disasters: A guide for primary care physicians.* Washington, DC: U.S. Department of Health and Human Services. Publication No. (SMA) 95-3022.

Jacobs, G., Quevillon, R., & Ofman P. (1998). Crisis intervention in the aftermath of aviation disasters. In L. VandeCreek, S. Knapp, & J. L. Jackson (Eds.), *Innovations in clinical practice* (Vol. 16, pp. 369–382). Sarasota, FL: Professional Resource Press.

Lindemann, E. (1944). Symptomatology and management of acute grief. *American Journal of Psychiatry, 101,* 141–148.

Mays, R. A., Jr. (1993, November). *Natural disasters and humanitarian operations: The federal social work response.* Paper presented at the meeting of the National Association of Social Workers, Orlando, FL.

McCammon, S. L., & Allison, E. J., Jr. (1995). Debriefing and treating emergency workers. In C. R. Figley (Ed.), *Compassion fatigue: Coping with secondary traumatic stress disorder in those who treat the traumatized.* New York: Brunner/Mazel.

McDonald, J. D., Caraway, S. J., Vickers, K. S., Pate, A. N., Hegstad, H. J., Westby, M., Decoteau, T., & Storey, A. (1998). The mental health response to the Red River flood of 1997. In L. Vandecreek, S. Knapp, & T. L. Jackson (Eds.), *Innovations in clinical practice* (Vol. 16, pp. 439–454). Sarasota, FL: Professional Resource Press.

Meichenbaum, D. (1985). *Stress inoculation training.* New York: Pergamon Press.

Mitchell, J. T. (1983, January). When disaster strikes . . . the critical incident stress debriefing process. *Journal of Emergency Services, 8*(1), 36–39.

Morgan, J. (1995). American Red Cross Disaster Mental Health Services: Implementation and recent developments. *Journal of Mental Health Counseling, 17* (3), 291–300.

Myers, D. G. (1994). *Disaster response and recovery: A handbook for mental health professionals.* (Substance Abuse & Mental Health Services Administration Publication No. SMA 94-3010). Rockville, MD: Center for Mental Health Services.

Pennebaker, J., & Sussman, J. (1988). Disclosure of traumas and psychosomatic processes. *Social Science and Medicine, 26,* 327–332.

Weaver, J. D. (1995). *Disasters: Mental health interventions.* Sarasota, FL: Professional Resource Press.

Weaver, J. D. (1996a). Disaster mental health services. In L. Grobman (Ed.), *Days in the lives of social workers.* Harrisburg, PA: White Hat Communications.

Weaver, J. D. (1996b). Disaster mental health. *http://ourworld. compuserve.com/homepages/johndweaver*

Weaver, J. D. (1999). How to assist in the aftermath of disasters and other life crises. In L. VandeCreek & T. L. Jackson (Eds.), *Innovations in clinical practice: A source book* (Vol. 17, pp. 397–411). Sarasota, FL: Professional Resource Press.

TABLE 2.1
Debriefing Session Handout

This session has been scheduled to help everyone come to terms with the thoughts and feelings that arose out of the recent tragic situation that you all faced. The format for the session is based upon the original critical incident stress debriefing (CISD) model put forth by Jeffrey Mitchell in 1983.

[Fill in the name of the sponsoring organization] has provided the workers who will serve as facilitators for today's debriefing. The session will probably last from 1 to 2 hours, and it will cover these six areas:

1. *Initial Phase.* Introductions, a discussion about confidentiality, an explanation of the purpose for holding the meeting, and a review of some other guidelines for the session. Some general rules, in addition to the need to maintain confidentiality, are:
   - Please speak only for yourself.
   - There is no rank during the session (i.e., no one is more important than anyone else).
   - No press and no outsiders are allowed to attend; this is for those who were directly involved. If you feel you do not belong in the session, please speak up about it right away.
   - Once we begin, there will be no break until we end the session.
   - Please turn beepers off and avoid phone calls (or any other interruptions) until we end.
   - This will not be an investigation or a critique.
   - Please plan to stay for the entire session.
   - No one has to talk if you do not want to do so.
   - Feel free to ask questions at any time.

2. *Fact Phase.* Review of what actually happened during and after the incident (e.g., exploring what each person saw, heard, smelled, touched, thought, and did during the crisis).

3. *Feeling Phase.* Review of the feelings each person had at the time of the incident and in the time since the incident.

4. *Symptom Phase.* Examination of the physical and psychological aftereffects of the incident and the subsequent start of the recovery period.

5. *Teaching Phase.* Reminder to everyone that the symptoms they are experiencing are normal responses to the abnormally stressful situation they have faced.

6. *Reentry Phase.* Wrap up, answer any final questions, and develop a plan for any future action(s) that may be needed.

We hope this debriefing is helpful to you as you continue with the recovery process. The facilitators welcome your questions and/or feedback about the session.

3

Understanding Children in Crisis
THE DEVELOPMENTAL ECOLOGICAL FRAMEWORK
Wanda K. Mohr

MORE THAN THREE DECADES OF EMPIRICAL INVESTIGATIONS have highlighted the enormous complexities involved in studying and intervening with children who have been traumatized and who are in crisis. As a result, child trauma and its outcomes can no longer be viewed in terms of simple cause-effect relationships. There is increasing recognition that any traumatic event, such as child maltreatment, is a heterogeneous phenomenon that varies with respect to type, frequency, severity, and chronicity (Manly, Cicchetti, & Barnett, 1994). In addition, the impact of these traumatic events is linked to the child's age and developmental status (Cicchetti & Lynch, 1993).

Moreover, the effects of crisis events are mediated by numerous features of the child's ecology, including poverty (Pelton, 1978), job and family instability (Wolfner & Gelles, 1993), parental stress and social isolation (Garbarino, 1985), and community violence (Osofsky, 1995). Together, these findings speak to the multidimensional nature of crisis, its sequelae, and the necessity of a comprehensive conceptual framework to guide both research and practice.

This chapter describes a theoretical perspective that addresses the complexity that we face in understanding the interplay of biological, psychological, social, and cultural forces, all of which must be taken into account when considering children in crisis. Viewing the sequelae of traumatic events through the lens of this perspective makes us aware of factors and connections that might otherwise remain invisible. Bringing these things to awareness and visibility may prevent us from disregarding potentially important opportunities for intervention.

A DEVELOPMENTAL ECOLOGICAL PERSPECTIVE

A developmental ecological perspective has been identified as a heuristic theoretical framework to address the complexity of maltreatment and trauma research (Belsky, 1993; National Research Council [NRC], 1993). This perspective allows for a more thorough and accurate examination of the influences of trauma on child development by simultaneously addressing child and environmental characteristics. This framework draws on and integrates a number of ecological and transactional models to explain how risk and protective factors at multiple levels of the child's ecology and prior development contribute to our understanding of the developmental consequences of exposure to trauma or crisis, as well as of the processes that underlie maladaptive and resilient outcomes.

THE DYNAMIC OF DEVELOPMENT

The concept of development is foundational to any research or intervention approach with children. Growth and development result from a continuous and complex interplay between heredity and environment. According to a developmental ecological framework, competencies in childhood develop across multiple domains and along a continuum of progressive stages as a function of transactions among child, caregiver, and environmental characteristics. Each developmental stage presents unique challenges that must be resolved in order for successful growth and adaptation to occur (Cicchetti, 1990). According to this theoretical perspective, any major childhood trauma can potentially disrupt the resolution of these developmental tasks. Therefore, the effects of child trauma are determined by the child's developmental stage and the particular tasks with which the child is grappling (Cicchetti & Lynch, 1993).

The Role of Contexts

As children develop, they play an ever more active role in an ever widening environment. Thus development can be understood only within the context in which it occurs. Thus this model underscores the importance of recognizing that child development is affected by the context in which development occurs. This perspective posits that contextual characteristics may enhance or impede a child's mastery of stage-salient competencies (Aber & Cicchetti, 1984; NRC, 1993). Therefore, in researching and intervening with children, it is critical to examine the role of proximal and distal aspects of the environment in mediating the effects of trauma, particularly as they relate to the resolution of critical developmental tasks (NRC, 1993).

According to Belsky (1980), four distinct system levels describe influences that operate in the child's environment. These systems were conceptualized initially by Urie Bronfenbrenner (1979) as subsystems within systems within larger systems, "as a set of nested structures, each inside the next, like a set of Russian dolls" (p. 22). The two most distal levels of the environment are the *macrosystem* and the *exosystem*. The macrosystem, which includes the beliefs and values of the culture, serves as the master blueprint for the ecology of human development and reflects the shared collective assumptions of a people about how things should be done, as well as the institutions that represent those assumptions. An example of a macrosystem concept (or variable) is religion, because it involves values, beliefs, a definition of the world, and a set of institutions that reflect these beliefs. The exosystem includes aspects of the community in which the family lives. An example of an exosystem variable might be the level of violence or, conversely, the level of positive parental involvement in a given community.

The more proximal levels of the environment are the *microsystem* and *ontogenic development*. These systems exert the most direct influences on child development. The microsystem includes the immediate settings in which the child exists, most notably the family home and school. The quality of the microsystem depends on its ability to sustain and enhance development and to provide a context that is emotionally validating and emotionally challenging (Garbarino, 1995).

Ontogenic development consists of child characteristics connected to the child's own development and adaptation. These factors, such as age, temperament, and physical health, can contribute to a child's response to a given crisis. For example, younger children are more vulnerable to injury than older children, and those with a more difficult temperament will react quite differently to a crisis than those with easy temperaments (Belsky, 1993). Moreover, experiences that could be tolerated by a 12-year-old child can literally destroy an infant (Perry, 1997).

Risk factors at each system level of the model influence whether negative sequelae will occur at a given level. In addition, factors within a given level can affect outcomes in surrounding levels of the model. At higher, more distal levels of the ecology, such as the macrosystem and the exosystem, risk factors may increase the likelihood of negative events, such as community violence, and occurrences in these environmental systems may influence what happens in the microsystem. Clearly, the prevalence of traumatic events, such as violence within a community, contributes to an increased likelihood of spousal violence, child maltreatment, and other trauma-inducing events. For example, poverty and unemployment, which are often concentrated in inner-city neighborhoods, can produce increased stress and frustration that may lead to violence at both the broader community level and the more intimate family level.

The manner in which children cope with the challenges posed by their environments is evidenced in their own ontogenic development. An increased exposure to crises at all ecological levels makes the successful resolution of stage-salient developmental issues more problematic for children (Cicchetti, 1989), resulting in an increased likelihood of negative developmental outcomes and psychopathology (Cicchetti, 1990). Conversely, such an ecological model of violence and its effects also helps to account for resilient outcomes in some children. The presence of protective factors at any level of the ecology may help to explain why some children display successful adaptation in the face of intense crises either within their communities or within families (Cicchetti, 1993; Richters & Martinez, 1993).

Coupled with this ecological perspective, an organizational understanding of development offers a powerful theoretical framework for investigating developmental outcomes and processes (Cicchetti, 1989). An organizational perspective focuses on the quality of integration both within and among the multiple domains of individual development. This approach conceives of development as comprising a number of age- and stage-relevant tasks. Although the relative salience of these tasks may decrease in relation to newly emerging issues, they remain important to adaptation over time (Cicchetti, 1989), and the successful resolution of an early stage-salient issue increases the probability of subsequent successful adjustment (Sroufe & Rutter, 1984). As each stage-salient issue reaches ascendancy, opportunities for growth and consolidation, as well as challenges associated with new vulnerabilities, arise. Thus an ever changing model of development is portrayed in which newly formed competencies or maladaptations may surface throughout the life course (Cicchetti, 1993). Because each stage-salient issue also entails reciprocal roles for caregivers, parental influence can either enhance or hamper a child's successful negotiation of these issues. Moreover, comprehensive early childhood protective factors have the potential to buffer children against adverse effects of trauma.

In addition to organizational principles of development, transactional principles speak to the role of children's interactions with their environments in development. In addition to the organizational process mentioned, these interactions must be taken into account in order to understand any developmental outcomes. Thus according to the principles of transaction that are part of this perspective, events during a child's development do not result from a single influential factor in a cause-and-effect manner. Instead, they are determined by multiple simultaneous influences. These influences occur at numerous levels and include child factors, as well as environmental factors.

Risk and Protective Factors

In the *developmental ecological framework*, risk and protective factors can be present at all system levels of the child's ecology. These can be either enduring or transient and short term, and they are thought to influence development at different stages. These factors may impede mastery of stage-salient competencies, or they can act as buffers in the event of traumas and crises. Investigators are only now beginning to approach development and subsequent psychopathology from the standpoint of these interactive factors.

Garmezy (1981) has described the role of such factors as dispositional attributes, environmental conditions, and positive events that can mitigate the effects of negative or traumatic experiences. Individual characteristics such as high intelligence, certain kinds of temperament, the ability to appraise a traumatic event cognitively, and relationships with significant people are all examples of factors that are thought to have a buffering or protective effect on children. Conversely, insecure attachment relationships, poor quality parent-child involvement, exposure to family or community violence, and biological parameters such as impulsivity are examples of factors that are thought to place children at greater risk for future psychopathology.

IMPLICATIONS FOR RESEARCH AND PRACTICE

The developmental ecological framework forces us to consider the concept of trauma beyond the narrow confines of the individual child. Considering the complexity of the pathways along which children develop, it is not surprising that there is little empirical research that provides clear support for one intervention approach versus another. However, there may be some basic principles for practitioners who are placed in the position of coming up with an intervention for a child who has suffered from a traumatic event.

First, intervention is far more likely to be effective if it operates from a conceptual framework that views a child as developing within a system of risk and protective factors. To be most effective, interventions should be individually designed to meet the needs of *this* child; they should be multidisciplinary; and they should be directed at multiple contexts depending on the specific needs of the child and his or her family. The goal of intervention must be to provide the mix and intensity of service that is individually appropriate.

Considering the unique needs of each child and his or her family, this means that "one size fits all" programs of intervention, such as those designed for psychiatric inpatient units or packaged by entrepreneurs, are of little value. It is critical that practitioners consider the developmental levels of children, their caregivers, and the family as a system in both their assessments and subsequent interventions.

It is critical that practitioners consider the developmental level of the child and family as a system in their assessment and intervention strategies. Moreover, they should assess the nature of exposure, its severity, and the duration of the trauma or crisis. Children who are directly exposed to violence and, to a lesser degree, who have knowledge of violence or crisis but do not directly witness it are at risk for symptomatology (Eth & Pynoos, 1994; Fitzpatrick & Boldizar, 1993). Random but purposive acts, such as the Oklahoma City bombing of 1995, or randomly occurring events such as natural disasters may produce trauma-related pathology and require one set of interventions (Ofman, Mastria, & Steinberg, 1995), whereas cumulative and prolonged traumas, such as those that result from prolonged abuse or warlike situations, may require very different approaches (Magwaza, Killian, Petersen, & Pillay, 1993; Sack, Clarke, & Seeley, 1995).

In addition to the child's trauma, the family may be stressed as well, not only as a result of the crisis but also because of its developmental stage as a system (for example, young, blended, recent divorce). Or the family may not "fit" the traditional mother-father-children picture, and grandparents or other family members may be the primary caregivers.

Service providers should also move beyond the notion of traditional, in-office, one-to-one counseling and move to reach out to mobilize formal and informal helping resources on behalf of the child. To be most effective, interventions should be a collaborative process between the family and the community. Once specific needs have been assessed, interventions will vary. They can and should be rendered by formal and informal systems of professionals, paraprofessionals, or volunteer groups. Informal systems, as part of the exosystem, are particularly important because they can provide the social support that traumatized children and their families need long after formal interventions have been discontinued. These exosystem supports are crucial to an empowerment philosophy (DiLeonardi, 1993).

Moreover, because of our increasingly culturally diverse population, there is a great need to increase cultural competency among caregivers. Risk and protective factors within a child's ecology may differ according to race and ethnicity (Gould, 1991; Sue, Arrendondo, & McDavis, 1992). Basic cultural competency is achieved when practitioners accept and respect difference; engage in ongoing cultural self-assessment; expand their diversity knowledge and skills; and adapt service models to fit the child's culture, situation, and perceived needs (Rauch, North, Rowe, & Risley-Curtiss, 1993). Cultural competency is the ability to understand, to the best of one's ability, the world-view of a child within his or her cultural context; and one must adapt practice and interventions accordingly.

Finally, a paradigmatic shift that is based on a competency orientation is being suggested increasingly by scholars as one that has most relevance for intervention with any special needs populations (Hatfield, 1994; Lefley, 1998). Recognizing that caregivers cannot erase the trauma that has occurred within the child's life and also recognizing that a pathology or deficiency approach to intervention has its limitations, this shift has prompted a movement away from a pathogenesis, disease-based model of care to a health-based competence model. In this approach families are not viewed as pathological, pathogenic, or dysfunctional but as basically healthy and adaptive. Because of parents' unique knowledge of and their history with their children, they are seen as potentially competent and as having something valuable to contribute to the therapeutic relationship. The emphasis in this therapeutic approach is not to focus on weaknesses, liabilities, and illness but rather to construct interventions based on strengths and resources. The goal of intervention is not the treatment of dysfunction but the empowerment of families so they may achieve mastery and control over their lives (Marsh, 1992). A competency-based orientation helps to build on a family's existing competencies and resources to respond to crises and stress, to meet needs, and to promote, enhance, and strengthen the functioning of the child and his or her family system.

REFERENCES

Aber, J. L., & Cicchetti, D. (1984). The social-emotional development of maltreated children: An empirical and theoretical analysis. In H. Fitzgerald, B. Lester, & M. Yogman (Eds.), *Theory and research in behavioral pediatrics* (pp. 176–191). New York: Plenum Press.

Belsky, J. (1993). Etiology of child maltreatment: A developmental-ecological analysis. *Psychological Bulletin, 114*(3), 413–434.

Bronfenbrenner, U. (1979). *The ecology of human development: Experiments by nature and design.* Cambridge, MA: Harvard University Press.

Cicchetti, D. (1989). How research on child maltreatment has informed the study of child development: Perspectives from developmental psychopathology. In D. Cicchetti & V. Carlson (Eds.), *Child maltreatment: Theory and research on the causes and consequences of child abuse and neglect* (pp. 439–451). New York: Cambridge University Press.

Cicchetti, D. (1990). The organization and coherence of socioemotional, cognitive, and representational development: Illustrations through a developmental psychopathology perspective on Down syndrome and child maltreatment. In R. Thompson (Ed.), *Nebraska Symposium on Motivation:* Socioemotional development: Current theory and research in motivation, vol. 36. (pp. 259–279). Lincoln, NE, University of Nebraska Press.

Cicchetti, D. (1993). Developmental psychopathology: Reactions, reflections, projections. *Developmental Review 13*, 471–502.

Cicchetti, D., & Lynch, M. (1993). Toward an ecological/transactional model of community violence and child maltreatment: Consequences for children's development. *Psychiatry, 56*, 96–118.

DiLeonardi, J. W. (1993). Families in poverty and chronic neglect of children. *Families in Society, 74*, 557–562.

Eth, S., & Pynoos, R. S. (1994). Children who witness the homicide of a parent. *Psychiatry of Interpersonal Biological Processes, 57*(4), 287–306.

Fitzpatrick, K. M., & Boldizar, J. P. (1993). The prevalence and consequences of exposure to violence among African-American youth. *Journal of the American Academy of Child and Adolescent Psychiatry, 32*(2), 424–430.

Garbarino, J. (1985). An ecological approach to child maltreatment. In L. H. Pelton (Ed.), *The social context of child abuse and neglect* (pp. 228–267). New York: Human Sciences Press.

Garbarino, J. (1995). *Raising children in a socially toxic environment.* San Francisco: Jossey-Bass.

Garmezy, N. (1981). Children under stress: Perspectives on antecedents and correlates of vulnerability and resistance to psychopathology.

In A. I. Rabin, J. Arnoff, A. M. Barclay, & R. A. Zucker (Eds.). *Further explorations in personality* (pp. 120–155). New York: Wiley.

Gould, K. H. (1991). Limiting damage is not enough: A minority perspective on child welfare issues. In J. E. Everett, S. S. Chipungo, & B. R. Leashore (Eds.), *Child welfare: An Africentric perspective* (pp. 58–78). New Brunswick, NJ: Rutgers University Press.

Hatfield, A. B. (1994). Family education: Theory and practice. In A. B. Hatfield (Ed.), *Family interventions in mental illness* (pp. 3–13). San Francisco: Jossey-Bass.

Lefley, H. P. (1998). The family experience in cultural context: Implications for further research and practice. In H. P. Lefley (Ed.), *Families coping with mental illness: The cultural context* (pp. 97–107). San Francisco: Jossey-Bass.

Magwaza, A. S., Killian, B. J., Petersen, I., & Pillay, Y. (1993). The effects of chronic violence on preschool children living in South African townships. *Child Abuse and Neglect, 17,* 795–803.

Manly, J. T., Cicchetti, D., & Barnett, D. (1994). The impact of subtype, frequency, chronicity, and severity of child maltreatment on social competence and behavior problems. *Development and Psychopathology, 6,* 121–143.

Marsh, D. (1992). *Families and mental illness: New directions in professional practice.* New York: Praeger.

National Research Council. (1993). *Understanding child abuse and neglect.* Washington, DC: National Academy of Sciences.

Ofman, P. S., Mastria, M. A., & Steinberg, J. (1995). Mental health responses to terrorism: The World Trade Center bombing. *Journal of Mental Health Counseling, 17* (3), 312–320.

Osofsky, J. D. (1995). The effects of exposure to violence on young children. *American Psychologist, 50,* 782–788.

Pelton, L. H. (1978). Child abuse and neglect: The myth of classlessness. *American Journal of Orthopsychiatry, 48,* 608–617.

Perry, B. D. (1997). Incubated in terror: Neurodevelopmental factors in the "cycle of violence." In J. Osofsky (Ed.), *Children in a violent society* (pp. 124–149). New York: Guilford Press.

Rauch, J. B., North, C., Rowe, C., & Risley-Curtiss, C. (1993). *Diversity competence: A learning guide.* Baltimore: University of Maryland School of Social Work.

Richters, J. E., & Martinez, P. (1993) NIMH community violence project: Children as victims of and witnesses to violence. *Psychiatry, 56,* 7–21.

Sack, W. H., Clarke, G., & Seeley, J. (1995). Post traumatic stress disorder across two generations of Cambodian refugees. *Journal of the American Academy of Child and Adolescent Psychiatry, 34*(9), 1160–1166.

Sroufe, L. A., & Rutter, M. (1984). The domain of developmental psychopathology. *Child Development, 55,* 17–29.

Sue, D. W., Arrendondo, P., & McDavis, R. J. (1992). Multicultural counseling competencies and standards: A call to the profession. *Journal of Multicultural Counseling, 20,* 64–88.

Wolfner, G. D., & Gelles, R. J. (1993). A profile of violence toward children: A national study. *Child Abuse and Neglect, 17,* 197–212.

Developmental Issues in Stress and Crisis

Wendy N. Zubenko

CHILDREN AND ADOLESCENTS EXPERIENCE AND RESPOND TO stress and crises in ways quite different from adults. Throughout this chapter, when I refer to children, the reader should understand that this includes adolescents as well, unless otherwise stated. This chapter describes children's responses to traumatic events and discusses warning signs that the child's usual way of coping is either no longer working or is unhealthy. Specific interventions are also discussed.

One needs only to pick up the daily paper or listen to the news to know that disasters and trauma (whether natural or brought on by humans) are not uncommon and are on the rise. The effects of these events are far-reaching and devastating for the entire community. Children have been identified as being among the most susceptible among the population to negative effects of trauma. The experience of trauma is unique to each child and affected by many different variables, including the child's developmental level, his or her own repertoire of healthy coping strategies, the amount of exposure to the trauma, and the reaction of the family and other adults. Effects appear to be greater when children experience loss or devastation (Newman,

1976), are directly exposed to the event (Bradburn, 1991), are separated from their parents, or see their parents react in a panicked manner (Bloch, Silber, & Perry, 1956).

NORMAL DEVELOPMENT

Understanding and appreciating the emotional and developmental levels of children and the developmental issues they are experiencing are extremely important first steps when assessing the impact of stress and crises. A well-established and accepted theory of childhood psychological development was formulated by E. H. Erikson (1964). He emphasized the importance of social and environmental factors in the home and community that influence psychological and personality development, and he described eight stages of development based on biological, psychological, and social events (Table 4.1). Another early pioneer, Harry Stack Sullivan (1953), developed what is considered the most comprehensive theory of the development of interpersonal relations. Sullivan theorized that personality development is determined within the context of interactions with others. He described six stages of personality development, which he divided according to the capacity for communication and integration of new experiences (Table 4.2). A third theory of development is Jean Piaget's (1952), which makes cognition a central focus. For Piaget, consciousness, judgment, and reasoning depend primarily on the individual's evolving intellectual capacity to organize experiences. In Piaget's theory the developing child passes through four stages, each reflecting a range of organizational patterns that occur in a definite sequence and within an approximate age span (Table 4.3).

As any parent of an adolescent will attest to, adolescence is a time of much change and turmoil as the young person strug-

TABLE 4.1
Erikson's Stages of Psychosocial Development

STAGE OF DEVELOPMENT	DEVELOPMENTAL TASK	MAJOR CHARACTERISTICS	SIGNS OF DYSFUNCTION
Birth to 12 months old	Trust versus mistrust	Mother figure viewed as significant	• Avoidant or ambivalent • Disorganization • Dysfunctional attachment
1 to 3 years old	Autonomy versus shame and doubt	Ego skills: parallel play, negativism; ambivalence; self-control and will-power; initial development of ego	• Avoids social interactions • Inability to show sadness or empathy • Lack of impulse control • Aggression • Self-doubt
3 to 6 years old	Initiative versus guilt	Cooperative play	• Poor sense of self-competency • Fails socially • Motor awkwardness • Lacks persistence • Poor sphincter control (soiling)
6 to 12 years old	Industry versus inferiority		• Dependent behavior • Lacks academic achievement • Difficulty establishing relationships • Inappropriate adjustment behaviors
12 to 18 years old	Identity versus identity diffusion		• Antisocial behaviors • Lacks healthy coping skills • Poor peer relationships • Somatic (physical) complaints

TABLE 4.2
Sullivan's Stages of Interpersonal Growth and Development

STAGE OF DEVELOPMENT	DEVELOPMENTAL TASK	INTERPERSONAL NEEDS
Infancy (birth to 18 months)	Learning to count on others to meet needs	Need for contact
Childhood (19 months to 6 years)	Learning to accept, in relative comfort, interference with wishes	Need for adult participation in activities
Juvenile (7 to 9 years)	Learning to form satisfactory relationships with peers	Need for peers Need for acceptance
Preadolescence (10 to 12 years)	Learning to relate to peer of same sex	Need for best friend or loved one
Early adolescence (13 to 14 years)	Learning to become independent Learning to establish satisfactory relationships with the opposite sex	Need for intimacy
Late adolescence (15 to 21 years)	Learning to become interdependent Learning to form durable sexual relationship with selected member of the opposite sex	Need for heterosexual relationship

TABLE 4.3
Piaget's Stages of Cognitive Development

STAGE OF DEVELOPMENT	CRITICAL EXPERIENCE	MAJOR CHARACTERISTICS
Sensorimotor (birth to 2 years)	Learning to recognize the permanence of objects	• Goal-directed behavior • Imitation in terms of make-believe
Preconceptual (3 to 4 years)	Symbolic mental activity Learning to think in terms of past, present, and future	• Egocentrism • Use of language as major tool of communication
Intuitive (5 to 7 years)	Learning to integrate concepts based on relationships	• Comprehension of basic rules • Increased exactness in imitation of reality
Concrete operations (8 to 11 years)	Learning to use logic and objectivity in concrete thought	• Classification of events • Reversibility
Formal operations (12 to 15 years)	Learning to think abstractly and logically	• Use of scientific approach to problem solving

gles to bridge the gap between being a child and becoming a mature adult. Each adolescent is unique in his or her approach to this task, but certain issues face all adolescents during their journey. The American Academy of Child and Adolescent Psychiatry (AACAP) has outlined the normal behaviors and feelings that most adolescents experience in middle school, early high school, late high school years, and beyond (AACAP, 1997a, 1997b). In *middle school* and the *early high school years*, adolescents experience:

Movement Toward Independence

- Struggle with sense of identity
- Feeling awkward or strange about oneself and one's body
- Focus on self, alternating between high expectations and poor self-concept
- Interests and clothing style influenced by peer group
- Moodiness
- Improved ability to use speech to express oneself
- Realization that parents are not perfect; identification of their faults
- Less overt affection shown to parents, with occasional rudeness
- Complaints that parents interfere with independence
- Tendency to return to childish behavior, particularly when stressed

Future Interests and Cognitive Changes

- Mostly interested in the present, limited thoughts of future

- Intellectual interests expand and gain in importance
- Greater ability to do work (physical, mental, emotional)

Sexuality

- Displays of shyness, blushing, and modesty
- Earlier physically development in girls than boys
- Increased interest in the opposite sex
- Movement toward heterosexuality with fears of homo-sexuality
- Concern regarding physical and sexual attractiveness to others
- Frequently changing relationships
- Worries about being normal

Morals, Values, and Self-Direction

- Rule and limit testing
- Capacity for abstract thought
- Development of ideals and selection of role models
- More consistent evidence of conscience
- Experimentation with sex and drugs

In *late high school* and beyond, adolescents experience

Movement Toward Independence

- Increased independent functioning
- Firmer and more cohesive sense of identity
- Examination of inner experience
- Ability to think ideas through
- Decrease in conflicts with parents
- Increased ability for delayed gratification and compro-mise

- Increased emotional stability
- Increased concern for others
- Increased self-reliance
- Continuing importance of, peer relationships, which take an appropriate place among other interests

Future Interests and Cognitive Changes

- More defined work habits
- Increased concern for the future
- More importance placed on one's role in life

Sexuality

- Feelings of love and passion
- Development of more serious relationships
- Firmer sense of sexual identity
- Increased capacity for tender and sensual love

Morals, Values, and Self-Direction

- Greater capacity for setting goals
- Interest in moral reasoning
- Capacity to use insight
- Increased emphasis on personal dignity and self-esteem
- Renewed importance of social and cultural traditions

CHILDREN'S SENSE OF LOSS, GRIEF, AND BEREAVEMENT

Loss and grief can mean many things for children and adolescents. Grief is most commonly associated with death, though we can grieve over the loss of anything that was important to us, such as a friendship, a home, physical health, a pet, a school, or a neighborhood. Children's understanding of loss and death and their responses are also developmental in nature. Because of their limited developmental capacities and their level of maturity, children often experience greater difficulty understanding, resolving, and managing their loss and grief. Infants and toddlers are unable to comprehend death and experience the loss often in terms of separation or abandonment. They perceive and are affected by the responses of their caretakers. Preschoolers view illness, loss, and death as punishment for some wrongdoing (real or imagined) and may view death as a sleep from which one awakens. Children in this age group shift between reality and fantasy, especially with regard to loss and death. They recognize that the people around them feel sad, worried, or frightened, and they too become frightened. Young school-age children (6 to 9 years old) often feel responsible for the events, loss, or death. They still possess magical thinking and may associate loss and death with witches, monsters, violence, mutilation, or punishment. Older school-age children (10 to 12 years old) realize that death is permanent and that everyone dies. They are curious about the specifics of the event and often will ask questions, such as "Was there blood splattered everywhere?" They are fascinated by the "shock" and "gory" aspects of the tragedy. Feelings of guilt are also common with these older children, and they will often bargain with themselves to become "perfect" in an effort to make up for the devastating loss. Adolescents may seem to have an adult view of death, but not an emotional view. They begin to acknowledge their own mortality. This can be very frightening for teenagers, and they may withdraw and deny the loss.

Most children who have experienced a traumatic event do not develop a specific psychiatric illness, though a significant number of children may display symptomatic behaviors. Most children will respond predictably to traumatic events and loss based on their age, developmental stage, and previous experiences (Table 4.4). The effects are greater when the child directly experiences the loss or devastation, or is separated from his or her parent(s) or when parent(s) react in an emotional, distressed, "panicked" manner. Many children exhibit increased fears and worries following traumatic events. Preschoolers often display changes in their behavior, such as an increase in the number and severity of problem behaviors displayed. They often cling more to parents, become demanding, whiny, irritable, and more easily frustrated, and have temper tantrums and sleep difficulties. Older children often report feeling more anxious and worried and have physical complaints of headaches and stomachaches, as well as school problems. Adolescents tend to exhibit withdrawal and avoidance, including refusing to attend activities associated with the event, blocking thoughts and feelings about the event, and using activities to promote distraction. This avoidance behavior facilitates denial of the reality of the tragedy and provides the adolescent protection from painful feelings that can seem overwhelming.

It is extremely important to recognize the effects of the trauma on the child and to intervene in ways that are supportive and age and developmentally appropriate, and that allow for the child to express his or her thoughts and feelings in a safe, nonjudgmental atmosphere. Often the children's problems, fears, experience, and reactions are overlooked while the family and other adults attend to the immediacy of the situation. This can lead to the child feeling rebuffed, sad, angry, confused, and frightened.

INTERVENTIONS

If we view trauma or loss as an abnormal event in the life of a child or adolescent, then one intervention goal should be to cre-

TABLE **4.4**
Responses to Loss, Grief, and Bereavement in Children and Adolescents

PRESCHOOLERS	SCHOOL AGE	ADOLESCENTS
Temper tantrums	Physical complaints, often headache and stomachache	Seek isolation
Crying	Sleep problems	Become less communicative
Clinging and demanding	Moodiness	Sleep problems, including withdrawal by increased sleep
"Scary" nightmares	Avoidance, apathy	School problems
Helplessness	Aggression	Feel different or alienated because of their experience
Disorganized behavior	School problems such as refusing to go to school, behavior problems, poor grades, poor concentration	Sadness, anger, irritability
Regressive behaviors, e.g., thumb sucking, bedwetting	Fears of darkness, sleeping alone, safety, separation from parent	Increased risk-taking behaviors
Moodiness, irritability	Anger, usually directed toward peers	May begin or increase substance use *(continued)*

TABLE 4.4 (continued)
Responses to Loss, Grief, and Bereavement in Children and
Adolescents

PRESCHOOLERS	SCHOOL AGE	ADOLESCENTS
Fears of darkness, crowds, strangers, being alone, separation from parent	Revert to the use of illogical and magical thinking	Avoidance of trauma-related thoughts, feelings, activities (including disaster mental health efforts)
Crying	Previously existing behaviors become extreme and exaggerated	Indifference
Easily frightened, followed by anger	Sadness, fear, worries about abandonment	Aggression (breaking objects, fighting, arguing, sometimes provoking fights)
Increased aggression, especially in boys	Boys display negative behaviors	Feelings of hopelessness, neglect, that no one cares
Impulsive behaviors	Girls display lack of self-competency	Belligerence, disobedience, talking back to parents or authority figures

ate a "normalizing environment" for the individual. This should
be done in conjunction with any other interventions that are
instituted. In many situations, normalizing activities alone can
have a dramatic impact on stabilizing a child during a time of
grief or trauma.

Return the child to a normal childhood routine as soon as
possible. This may include educational activities, recreational
activities, routine bedtimes, sports, clubs, parties, and family

customs such as sharing meals together. Children respond more favorably when they are in an environment that provides them with the security of familiar activities. Children need to be given permission to do the job of children, with opportunities specifically for learning and playing. Chapter 5 discusses the importance of play and the therapeutic use of play for children who experience trauma.

Intervention counselors should provide a safe opportunity for children to discuss their thoughts and feelings; answer questions honestly about the event, trauma, or loss; and offer acceptable, healthy outlets for expression. It is important to acknowledge the frightening and sad aspects of the trauma when talking with a child, but one must be careful not to overwhelm the child. Often, with the best of intentions, adults believe that the children are experiencing the trauma in the same way as the adult and attempt to help the children through adult rituals. Children should be given a choice of whether or not to attend funerals and memorial services. Having "counseling sessions" at every activity that the child encounters (at school, at church, in the community, and also at club meetings) can add to the child's sense of fear.

Helping Children Cope

The following is a brief list of ways in which we can help children and adolescents cope in a healthy manner during times of major stress:

- Get the children back into a *normal routine* as soon as possible.
- *Listen carefully* to what the child has to say. Show interest, concern, and sincerity.
- Be *patient and honest*. Children often have difficulty ex-

pressing themselves verbally; let them express themselves in their own way (as long as it is not dangerous).

- Provide *opportunities in which the child or adolescent has control*. Let them make some decisions. In a tragedy or disaster, control is taken away from all of us. Helping the child to regain some sense of control over his or her environment and life is very important.
- *Facilitate age and developmentally appropriate discussion among children* about the event, loss, or tragedy. Provide a forum to educate and to *normalize the experience*. This can be especially helpful for adolescents, for whom the peer group is very important.
- Allow the children to *tell and retell their stories*, including the painful details that you would rather avoid. You can use this as an opportunity to provide education and support.
- Provide children an *opportunity to "say good-bye"* and to resolve their feelings about the loss.
- Help them *focus on immediate problem solving*.
- Be a *role model* in managing stress, in problem solving, and in exhibiting healthy coping skills.
- Provide for non-trauma-related activities. *Have fun.*
- Encourage and utilize help from *support groups*, such as peer groups, school, church, and so forth.

When To Get Help
When in doubt, always seek assistance. Keep the following points in mind:

- Any time a child or adolescent is in danger of harming him- or herself or others, immediately seek the assistance of a professional.

- If the behaviors are persistent and show no evidence of gradually improving, seek assistance.

Look for the following problems. If any are present, seek help:

- If the child persistently refuses school or if grades drop with no improvement noted
- If a child loses all interest or pleasure in activities that used to be pleasurable
- If the child talks about hurting or killing himself or herself
- If the child withdraws completely from family and friends or is noncommunicative
- If there is any evidence that the child is hearing or seeing things that others do not experience
- If the child is unable to eat or sleep enough to remain healthy

REFERENCES

American Academy of Child and Adolescent Psychiatry. (1997a, May). Normal adolescent development: Middle school and early high school years. *Facts for families,* Retrieved from http://www.aacap.org/publications/factsfam/develop.htm

American Academy of Child and Adolescent Psychiatry (1997b, May). Normal adolescent development: Late high school years and beyond. *Facts for families,* Retrieved from http://www.aacap.org/publications/factsfam/develop2.htm

Bloch, D. A., Silber, E., & Perry, S. E. (1956). Some factors in the emotional reaction of children to disaster. *American Journal of Psychiatry, 113,* 416–422.

Bradburn, I. (1991). After the earth shook: Children's stress symptoms 6–8 months after a disaster. *Advances in Behavioral Research and Therapy, 13,* 173–179.

Erikson, E. H. (1964). *Childhood and society* (2nd. ed.). New York: Norton.

Newman, C. J. (1976). Children of disaster: Clinical observations of Buffalo Creek. *American Journal of Psychiatry, 133,* 306–312.

Piaget, J. (1952). *The origin of intelligence in children.* New York: International Universities Press.

Sullivan, H. S. (1953). *Interpersonal theory of psychiatry.* New York: Norton.

Posttraumatic Stress Disorder and Reaction

June A. Esser

To be understood is a luxury
Ralph Waldo Emerson

THE TASK OF THIS CHAPTER IS TO EXPLAIN POSTTRAUMATIC stress disorder (PTSD) and posttraumatic stress reaction (PTSR), as well as to offer useful interventions for youth exposed to catastrophic events. In responding to the catastrophe, the helper must realize that PTSD and PTSR are only two of many possibilities that may manifest in the young person. PTSD and PTSR are diagnostic terms used in clinical and psychological settings. These terms allow mental health professionals to communicate about treatment. This diagnostic category was labeled and utilized (Charney, Deutch, Krystal, Southwick, & Davis, 1993) at a time when the community mental health movement had lost momentum. Addressing PTSD and PTSR in the community and outside the clinical setting represents a new intervention area. For the most part, individuals suffering with PTSD and PTSR receive the majority of attention when they are in crisis and exhibiting extreme or severe discomfort. The daily suffering and the internal turmoil endured by a person on an ongoing basis generally goes without notice.

The importance of sensitivity on the part of the helper cannot be stressed enough. The helper is first a human being with his or her own history of loss, trauma, and coping tendencies. Therefore, self-awareness and personal development remain priorities for all helpers. Peer support and feedback are key to this process.

PTSR is used to explain a cluster of possible symptoms. Over time, however, when the symptoms are experienced together, they represent an extreme negative outcome of exposure to trauma. This sustained and repeated experience of symptoms is termed PTSD. A detailed collection of scientific studies is summarized by Amaya-Jackson and March (1995) for the reader who wants more information on this disorder in children and adolescents.

The following definitions and descriptions (American Psychiatric Association, 1994) will help guide the reader through this chapter's discussion:

- *Catastrophic Event (CE)*. The event that has provoked and set into motion the process of disruption and reaction to the child's or adolescent's usual manner of living and daily experience.
- *Trauma*. The psychological, physical, and spiritual effects of the CE on the child's or adolescent's pattern of living.
- *Helper*. Individual with the desire to reach out in compassion to a child or adolescent who has experienced a catastrophe.
- *Post-Traumatic Stress Disorder*. Exposure to an event—either (experienced or witnessed directly or confronted sec-

ondhand by the child—that involves actual or threatened death or serious injury (to self or others) accompanied by feelings of extreme fear and helplessness. Children may exhibit agitated or disorganized behavior as an expression of the intense fear or horror.

- In addition, at least one of the following experiences must persist for at least 1 month:

    a. Intrusive reexperiencing of the event. Young children may express this reexperiencing by using themes or aspects of the trauma in their play.

    b. Recurrent and distressing dreams of the trauma. Children often experience very frightening dreams that have no recognizable content.

    c. Feeling or acting as if the traumatic event were happening again. Young children may reenact the trauma in their play and behavior.

    d. Psychological distress or physical reactions when exposed to cues that symbolize or resemble an aspect of the trauma. Examples of this type of cue include hearing police siren, seeing a fire truck, experiencing lightning or high winds (if the trauma was related to a storm or hurricane).

- When people are experiencing PTSD, they also persistently avoid stimuli associated with the trauma and may experience a general numbness. Examples of problematic behavior include:

    a. Avoiding thoughts, conversations, or feelings associated with the trauma.

    b. Avoiding activities, places, or people that arouse recollection of the trauma.

    c. Inability to recall important aspects of the trauma.

  d. Little, if any, interest in important activities and re-
     fusal to participate in these activities.
  e. Feeling estranged, separate, or detached from others.
  f. Inability to have a range of feelings (e.g., love, anger,
     sadness).
  g. Inability to imagine a future. Often people will talk
     about not expecting to live a normal life span or to
     have relationships, children, or a career.
- Other, physical, indications of PTSD include:
  a. Sleep difficulties, especially problems falling or staying
     asleep.
  b. Problems concentrating, forgetfulness, poor memory.
  c. Irritability, short temper, angry outbursts.
  d. Feeling tense, unable to relax.
  e. Startling easily.
- The signs and symptoms of PTSD cause impairment in
  important areas of life, such as schoolwork, relationships
  with parents or friends, or initiation of age-related tasks
  and responsibilities. PTSD symptoms persist for at least 1
  month and may become chronic, lasting for years.
- *Posttraumatic Stress Reaction*. The immediate experience of
  the symptoms of PTSD without the time lapsed between
  the CE and the present to determine whether the symptoms
  will persist or reoccur in the future. PTSR usually refers to
  symptoms or experiences like those in PTSD that have not
  persisted for at least 1 month. This difference also may be
  a function of the helper-helped relationship. For example,
  those who respond immediately to an event or are first on
  the scene may have a short-term relationship with those
  traumatized and therefore not have an the opportunity to
  know whether symptoms will persist or escalate.

WELLNESS PROMOTION

When a traumatic event occurs and news of the event spreads, we usually respond with shock and sadness. The response of the community contributes to an individual's interpretation of the trauma. Shock and sadness convey fear and hopelessness. Although these reactions and feelings are quite understandable, it is necessary for those who intend to act as helpers to suspend their own thoughts and feelings of fear, shock, sadness, and hopelessness. The intent to act and assist defies the hopelessness and testifies to the promise of change. When a helper steps out of the automatic, mechanical reaction and consciously decides to assist, he or she has already demonstrated evidence of transformation. The helper then shares the transformation with those he or she is assisting. The benefits of this transformation are often heard in the words of those assisted when they report the healing effect of just having another present in their pain. Levine (Levine & Frederick, 1997) defines transformation in terms of a returned capacity for nervous system self-regulation. Immobility is replaced with fluidity and fear with courage and perceptual changes of increased receptivity.

The ability to transcend the tendency to see the injustice and to dwell on the pain illustrates the human potential present in each of us. This human potential contains the energy that can be healing and real to those traumatized. Human suffering is our subject matter, and its complexity calls for an examination of what suffering actually entails. The following discussion explores physical, psychological, and spiritual needs in the wake of trauma.

PHYSICAL NEEDS

The body is the encasement and container of feelings, memories, sensations, and reactions to daily living. Neurological and hormonal responses affect our experience of trauma and are created by our processing of trauma (for the reader interested in more specific information concerning the central nervous system and its involvement in trauma exposure, see Charney et al., 1993). The musculoskeletal system is regulated by hormonal and neurological processes in the body. And because the muscuoskeletal system is responsible for mobility, posture, and observable functioning, it is possible to gain insight into how children are processing an event by how they move their bodies. For both the school-age child and the adolescent, the focus on outward physical appearance also can give an indication of underlying trauma if dress and habits disintegrate after exposure to such an event. A child's gait, coordination, and care in choosing clothing and grooming indicate a child's state of mind and can influence the reaction of peers. A traumatized child may need gentle reminders about physical appearance to prevent rejection from peers. Exercise and the need for mastery over the body remain critical as the child reorganizes behavior (see Table 5.1). In addition, a lack of synchronicity of body movements may exist as the psychological struggles for equilibrium continue to make performance demands. So it remains important that principles of safety in play and work be emphasized to avoid accidental injury. Helpers should also closely monitor traumatized children, as they may become distracted, clumsy, and careless at school and play.

Principles of wellness continue to be important throughout the reorganization period. Children may have to be coached in the need for adequate rest and leisure. This is particularly true when usual adult caregivers (parents, extended family, school personnel, and clergy) are also victims of the event. Helpers may need to create opportunities for the age-appropriate expression of physical activity and relaxation. Preoccupied and distracted adult caregivers can overlook this need and temporarily forget about those activities that are natural and necessary for normalization.

Similarly, the impact of adequate nutrition in a setting that is comforting and sustaining to the child's daily demands cannot be overemphasized. Consumption of regular meals in an environment which fosters conversation, sharing of daily concerns, and questions must continue in spite of catastrophic events.

PSYCHOLOGICAL NEEDS

In addressing the psychological aspects of PTSD and PTSR, specific areas of functioning can serve as indicators of mental health and targets of intervention. The will, the emotions, the imagination, the intellect, and the memory of the child all need to be considered and addressed (see Table 5.2). Each of these elements of mental life is dynamic and ever changing and can be altered in developing youngsters in response to trauma. For helpers, this both presents a challenge and opens the terrain for awe-inspiring change and growth. It is a challenge because helpers, enthusiastic about structuring an intervention in a particular way, may find it necessary to redesign midstream. A needs assessment may no longer fit what the child sees as a problem or a possibility over time. It remains important that helpers do not become overly attached to a specific outcome. The child may generate a new direction, which then accurately identifies the psychic injury and how the child might truly be helped. Breggin (1991) argues that PTSD is a helpful diagnosis because it actually evaluates

TABLE 5.1
Guidelines for Caregivers Responding to the Physical Needs of Youth Experiencing Trauma

- Maintain regular physical exercise for diversion and stimulation of bones and muscles to ensure healthy growth and manage stress.
- Maintain good principles of hygiene and infection control (e.g., regular and frequent hand washing, routine grooming).
- Apply principles of personal safety to prevent accidental injury.
- Educate caregivers about the sustaining effects of planned and nutritious meals.
- Encourage the rituals of meals, food selection, table rules, and meal-related chores to be continued as part of the child's routine.
- Encourage conversations that elicit humor, laughter, and diversions.
- Do not limit the child's expression of negative feelings or fears during meals.
- Encourage adults to discipline consistently and not begin to compromise rules to offset observable pain in the child.
- Continue household responsibilities and chores as much as possible, recognizing that some flexibility may be needed in light of the event.

the person's response to a life event. Therefore, the importance for an accurate assessment is clear. The personal meaning of trauma and its unique expression will differ from person to person.

The Will

A child's motivation and decision-making ability are powerful forces that operated fully before the crisis. Helpers sometimes have the advantage of being acquainted with a child before a disaster strikes or of having the opportunity to learn about the child's background from parents or caregivers.

If known, or once discovered, these details must be integrated into any plan to help. To ignore the child's natural tendencies and temperament will make the helper's task more difficult. If these things are unknown, the helper can gain insight by observing the child for his or her willingness to listen or to help others, the ability to delay gratification, the treatment of younger or more vulnerable children, and his or her approach to competition or game playing. Does the child seem to integrate issues of friendship, or is fairness the most prominent concern in problem solving? What is the child's relationship to authority figures? Is he or she both independent and dependent on others? Is there any imbalance toward one or the other? How do other children include or not include the child in play?

Answers to these questions can indicate something about the child's will and tendencies forward self and others. An excellent format to consider in discerning a child's type is detailed by Tieger and Barron-Tieger (1997). Using the four dichotomies of extravert-introvert, sensing-intuition, thinking-feeling, and judging-perceiving, the authors examine 16 personality possibilities and how to best embrace their tendencies. With traumatized children, the helper will be better equipped to assist if interventions are aligned with personality traits, such as the will.

The Emotions

The emotions are internal signals that reveal how and what the child may be processing about the event. The emotions are displayed in posture, facial expressions, activity level, and the child's ability or inability to verbalize certain feelings to the helper and others. Emotion identification may need to be taught. Children can be taught that feelings assist us in deciding what is loved and what is feared. They are like traffic signs because they do not instruct us where to go, but how we might get there safely. A child can be taught to discuss and to ask others about feelings and not to completely rely on feelings to make decisions.

Like road signs, feelings provide some of the information we need.

The Imagination

The imagination is the human capacity to mentally create a world beyond that which one has experienced, understands, or has been taught. The imagination serves to create what cannot be seen, tasted, heard, touched, or smelled in the immediate environment. Like the other elements of our mental life, the imagination presents opportunities and obstacles to wellness. What the child has experienced, understands, or has been taught can affect his or her capacity to imagine during the crisis. Some children's imaginative abilities are apparent in storytelling, play, and conversation. But not all children exhibit these abilities. For these children, a calm, relaxed setting may be necessary before the imagination can emerge. For the traumatized child, the ability to be spontaneous can be curative.

In whatever degree imagination exists, the goal remains to detect the form and purpose the imagination serves in the child's life. This may be achieved by offering an open-ended story or by inquiring how one has fun if one feels like being silly. Role-playing—with or without the helper's participation—using puppets or dolls can be very helpful for detecting a child's comfort level with creating new ideas. Ultimately, the level of spontaneity and willingness to assume new roles or generate unconventional ideas will be related to real-life problem solving. Traumatized youth often need coaching to increase confidence, and the imagination is a gateway to skill building. What can be imagined can be molded and reshaped so that it can be used in real-life settings. Without imagination, rigidity sets in and options are limited, leading to hopelessness.

TABLE 5.2
Guidelines for Caregivers Responding to the Emotional Needs of Youth Experiencing Trauma

- Feelings can happen suddenly, and more than one feeling can occur at a time.
- Feelings can change, and events can make feelings change.
- Feelings do not control us but are just one part of who we are.
- All people have feelings and experience all feelings at some time.
- We can talk about feelings.

The Intellect

The intellect includes the ability to process information and use it toward some goal. It includes, but is not limited to, what is formally taught, how it is made useful internally, and how it is exercised in the external world with others in relationships. The complicated nature of human intelligence sets the human experience apart from that of all other life forms. If and when the intellect becomes disorganized and out of touch with its unique position and, responsibility, a dulling and lack of enthusiasm are manifested, and hopelessness sets in.

In traumatized children, intellectual difficulties can take several forms, including apathy, rebellion, preoccupation with analyzing events, gathering facts or solving problems, and pseudomaturity. In reaching out, helpers should look for and promote balance in each individual child. This balance occurs when a curiosity for new information does not eliminate or minimize the need for affiliation with others in the child's environment. For instance, a traumatized child may become enthusiastic about a prominent sports celebrity. In studying the celebrity's life, the child collects pictures and statistics about his or her performance, and the child may spend a great deal of time imagining what it would be like to be famous. The critical factor is whether these cognitive processes become extreme and consume excessive time, significantly reducing the child's contact with peers. In this case, the child is using the intellect for escapism. The helper needs to determine to what degree and at what cost to other needs this escapism is occurring. It would also be very helpful to know the child's level of intellectual performance prior to the trauma and to know the level of involvement of the parents and school system in the crisis. Alterations in the behavior of parents and teachers may have a profound effect on a child's ability to cope in the present and to perform in the future. Helpers need to remember that assisting the permanent caregivers also may help the child. Education about child development, parents' fears and concerns, and other basic care issues may need to be reinforced during the crisis.

Memory

As with all dimensions of the child, memory offers a tremendous resource for healing. Each interaction, each social exchange of the past, is stored and possesses some potential to be retrieved at a later time. It becomes the foundation on which the child approaches experience, as it represents that which the child understands about the self and his or her everyday world. New discoveries, new challenges, and even daily rituals are approached and carried out through memory.

Consequently, historical data, as well as the timing of the trauma, create the impact of the event. Questions to consider include all the losses the child experienced at the time of the event. What successes was the child experiencing and have they changed because of the event? The child brings his or her entire self to the event. Memories that represent adaptation can promote additional mastery and can sustain the child at the time of the trauma. Likewise, consciously or unconsciously, previous exposure to loss that was not resolved can reemerge and undermine current efforts to manage the event.

If the relationship allows, a timeline review of the child's life may be helpful. Timeline reviews are conducted twice, once with the child and once with an adult caregiver or parent. For the child, the review may be initiated by asking what the child's earliest memories are. This question can be followed by asking whether this memory is the first thing they can recall. In general, children are able to talk about themselves and enjoy it.

The elasticity of the human brain represents unbounded possibilities and so can positively influence the management of the event at hand. The helper should keep in mind that current efforts may not be measurable at this time. The reason is that the human memory continues to interpret, react, store, and retrieve past experiences endlessly. Helpers initiating relationships with traumatized children will gauge their interventions according to the anticipated length of the relationship, as well as the child's tolerance for a relationship.

Practically speaking, the helper does not absolutely need to elicit or request a recall of past events but simply needs to be with the child in the present. If the helpers are fully present and allow themselves to respond, they will discover a rich terrain of experience. Fears, concerns, and myths from past injuries will erupt and provide a laboratory for adding to the memory base. Specifically, this is an opportunity for the child to rework the management of loss. These opportunities present themselves in the ordinary routines of eating, bathing, sleeping, playing, reading, exercising, and prayer.

As with all aspects of the child, it remains important to limit the amount of generalization that is applied to memory. Its utility in healing is driven by the complexity of the nervous system, the unique history of the child, and the management of the traumatic events. In addition, the helpers must be willing to modify their assumptions and conclusions if they become awkward and incongruent with the child's ongoing behaviors and reactions. A child may offer verbal or nonverbal feedback that communicates that the intervention is not helpful. Ironically, the empathic response to this feedback can be therapeutic. In accepting failure, the helper should not be discouraged, and the exchange can be transformed into another opportunity.

SPIRITUAL NEEDS

To understand and discover the spirit in the traumatized child, helpers must draw on their own self-study and conclusions about themselves. It is unlikely that any helper would be inspired to work with traumatized children unless he or she was already spiritually aware and his or her own spiritual development was a priority for self-growth. Specifically, it is the recognition of the spirit in one self that manufactures both the compassion and the hope conveyed to trauma victims in often hideous circumstances.

A basic assumption that most of us hold is that the spiritual self allows and sustains the body and mind. Therefore, when body or mind (psyche) is injured, the spiritual self can be called on to heal and repair the wounds. The spiritual dimension of human experience can be seen as a force—the least understood, but the most important to understand. It is what keeps us going when everything is falling apart. Children seem to understand the unlimited possibilities of the divine and embrace the potential more openly than adults do. From a cognitive perspective, the absence or limited expression of abstract thinking allows children to forgive more easily, to overlook others' shortcomings, and to stay focused in the present. Without the futuristic focus, children benefit from ordinary and everyday happenings. Because they are not burdened with worry and anxiety about the future, children are more receptive to the world around them. Consequently, they appreciate the sacred in the ordinary. For example, take an outdoor walk with a child and appreciate how much more he or she observes and experiences because of his or her openness. A child can quickly move between admiring the incline of a hill to noticing a group of insects involved in some cooperative effort.

In the traumatized child, this spontaneity, willingness, agility, enthusiasm, and ability to recall and integrate past enjoyments may or may not be impaired. The helper need not focus on the degree to which this is true but should focus on the task of supporting the reemergence of this response and the continuing to enjoyment of everyday experiences. This occurs when the helper models the behavior and acts as a participant in the experience. If opportunities are limited, the helper may need to craft exercises with art, story making, storytelling, or small plays to strongly suggest that the experience still exists and is within reach. Again, the ability to execute this behavior lies in the helper's willingness to let go of the pain of the present and observe the sacred in ordinary life.

It is important that helpers not rely on verbal techniques to promote healing. Children do not have the verbal skills, abstract thinking, or experiences on which to draw to allow the helper to enter their state of understanding. Helpers must be willing to meet the child at the level at which he or she understands the event. Techniques are paced and driven by what the child reports as helpful, good, or fun. A comparison can be made to a budding plant. If a rough storm comes along and showers bring excessive rain and strong winds that eliminate the soil, the need for sunshine to generate more buds becomes a secondary need. The foundation needs attention first, and so it is with trauma in the life of a child. Repair is aimed at the foundation; the need for soil in which to grow strong stems is primary. Spontaneity, enthusiasm, and willingness are prerequisites to future healing. Often verbal expression occurs later.

Many believe that in returning to the sacred, we can observe an order to human development, which was engineered for a purpose. Spontaneity, enthusiasm, willingness, and the ability to enjoy the simple things in life are mastered in childhood. But adults can maintain these attributes and apply them to stressors long after they acquire language skills, critical thinking, and well-developed impulse control. Adults cope better because all these attributes of childhood continue to serve a vital function which cannot be ignored. Why the Divine decided to construct us in this manner is a mystery.

However, the design will not tolerate rearranging, and helpers will observe that traumatized youth begin to eliminate core elements of spontaneity, which are difficult to recover. Spontaneity cannot be replaced with mechanical talk and verbalizations about the pain. If spontaneity is lost, the end result often is depression, anxiety, boredom, and somatization. Consequently, interpersonal relationships suffer due to irritability, withdrawal, and an inability to relax. The traumatized child loses affiliation and relations with others. The absence of spontaneity continues, and the cycle gains momentum as it feeds on itself. Viktor Frankl, in his popular book *Man's Search for Meaning*, discusses the need to define life's meaning as a primary need for the individual (Frankl, 1984). Care must be taken to reduce mechanical interventions that do not honor the dynamic nature of the child.

Several cases follow in which we can see how specific children reacted to traumas they experienced.

CASE STUDIES

The following excerpts from my clinical notes are offered to illustrate some of the concepts presented in this chapter that will help the child with symptoms of PTSD to heal.

Introduction

The three male children described here are biological brothers. They all experienced the same catastrophic event—their father's death in an airplane crash. Their father worked out of town often and traveled frequently. One day he went to work and did not return. Because 132 persons died in the crash with many unanswered questions as to why, the aftermath was tremendously complicated. There was internal turmoil and confusion in the family. There was the involvement of external factors such as the media (television and newspapers, local and national) and legal issues. After 5 years, this well-publicized tragedy continues to receive intermittent coverage in both local television and newspapers.

Case 1

James, also known as *Jamie*, was 8 years old at the time of the event. He is the oldest son and his father's namesake.

Key Information. Jamie was a pensive boy who remained guarded and thoughtful before each response. He was most concerned about his mother, and much of his conversation centered around this worry. When I attempted to engage him in play, he remained tense and preoccupied. If his brothers were present, he developed a pseudomature posture and began to "parent" them. If he was seen individually, he focused on what his brothers had done to upset his mother recently. Jamie was unable to relax at home or school. He preferred to think about schoolwork a lot, even if he thought he gave his best effort. He was of above average intelligence. His mom reported that he had always been hypervigilant, but his irritability and somatization increased after his father was killed.

Interventions and Helper Strategies. Attempts to soothe Jamie with play or distraction were largely unsuccessful. Although only 8 years old, Jamie quickly transformed his time with me into conversations. He was often restless and would gaze away as he offered his ideas on various topics. Most conversations would start with my asking about how he was coping and would end with Jamie weaving his own understanding of others and their involvement. For instance, when discussing school progress, Jamie would move the discussion to the positive and negative attributes of a particular teacher. Often this review would come full circle and back to the kind of person he was or wanted to be, the kind of person his mom was and often the kind of person his dad was.

For Jamie, his ability to apply his intellect was critical to his healing. The disorganization and confusion of the catastrophic event were best stabilized by exercising his gifts of reason. I was required to yield my ideas regarding therapeutic play because this child did not find comfort in the buffering of play. His need to express the anxiety and discomfort made the most of his dominant tendency to reason. His memory complemented and supported his preferences. My job was to guide his intellect and memory in support of creating new experience. This new experience would create new memories that could be recalled as a time when he was embraced for all that he was, a bright and sensitive boy who sorted through a catastrophe with careful reasoning ability.

Termination. As expected, Jamie created his own termination plan, which allowed him time to think and analyze our relationship. He first suggested that he would let me know when he wanted to meet with me. He gradually increased the time between meetings and then just accompanied his youngest brother to oversee those meetings. He gradually decided he did not need to keep meeting with me because he was okay.

Case 2

Matthew, also known as Matt, was 7 years old at the time of the event, a boy who learned and came to understanding by doing.

Key Information. Matt was bored and annoyed with any attention to his feelings and preferred to spend time in competitive play. At times, he would become frustrated and then abruptly report his feelings, but he did not find it helpful to elaborate on them. Although he was the most verbal about his dad's death, his comments did not reflect his sadness or fear. His comments were angry and primarily descriptive regarding the accident and how he perceived his family in the crisis. In play, he was always in favor of changing rules or discussing whether they could be altered or at least temporarily suspended. His imagination was vivid, and his emotions often strong. The added activity of dealing with the catastrophe seemed to overstimulate Matt. His usual ability to juggle his active imagination, emotions, and will seemed to hit a wall, and he was uncomfortable.

Interventions and Helper Strategies. For me to be of service to this child, it was important to maintain some structure for our time together. However, rigid application would certainly increase the confusion for this energetic child. Therefore, rules were made and stated at each meeting. It was understood that multiple prompts would result in time-out, during which he would receive no attention. He was given control of the type of play activity and the length of play time. I consciously inserted a flexible schedule.

I became aware of the importance of my own nonverbal messages, especially if they conveyed nonacceptance. I did this because Matt had a vivid imagination and big emotions that he was attempting to organize in the relationship, and he did not need any additional material to work into the maze.

Termination. At one point, Matt became furious about limit setting and refused to work with me any more. I gently invited him to consider whether that was what he really wanted and told him that if he changed his mind, he was always welcome back into the relationship. He did return, although not right away. After a time, he was open to negotiating his termination, and he did so without resentment.

Case 3

Joshua, also known as Joshie, was 4-1/2 years old at the time of the event.

Key Information. Because of his age and because he was the youngest of the three brothers, Joshie was a follower at the time of his father's death. He often sat on his oldest brother's lap and would mimic his words or expressions Joshie would show enthusiasm and emotion for play as his brothers did, displaying a desire to sometimes change activities with his brothers. His strongest reactions to his dad's death occurred when viewing family photographs and his brothers' artwork, as well as when he began creating his own artwork. He was attentive to his brothers' words and especially to his mother. He became very clingy with mom at this time.

Interventions and Helper Strategies. I have met with Joshie intermittently over the past 5 years. He is no longer a follower but has developed his own opinions, which he uses in relating and responding to me. He is beginning to put memories into a framework that will allow him to understand his loss. He is receptive to feeling identification and is beginning to develop his own identity and a sense of his place in the catastrophic past. As he recalls and integrates the past, he uses the memories of a 4-1/2-year-old boy and those of his family as told from their experience. I provide a consistent presence of one who has been with him throughout his development.

Summary of Cases

Promoting wellness following a catastrophic loss can alleviate, lessen, or eliminate symptoms of PTSR and the development of PTSD. In the cases reviewed, there were clear psychological differences between the three brothers. The will, emotions, imagination, intellect, and memory can be more or less active and therefore dominant in different children. Regardless of the dominant feature, the need for normalization and acceptance is primary. It is noteworthy that, in considering the physical and spiritual domains, more similarities were noted among the brothers.

All three boys are athletes and active in team sports, especially hockey, a passion of their dad's. Their mother was supportive of their athletic efforts and promoted team involvement.

And, from a spiritual perspective, all three boys believed their dad was in heaven. Early artwork and conversations often came to this conclusion. In more recent conversations this belief continues and provides a sense of peace.

I do not suggest any conclusions about prognosis or outcome based on these relationships. It has been postulated that over time, PTSD is a chronic and disabling condition. However, predictions are limited by the poorly designed studies of psychotherapy and the possibility that treatments need to be tailor-made for specific types of trauma (Roth & Fonagy, 1996).

The aftermath of the trauma continues to unfold in the lives of these three boys. Unfinished legal matters contribute to a lack of closure. Anniversary dates and birthdays bring the emotional recollections a little closer to the surface, but life goes on.

Note: The children involved requested that their real names be used in this writing. Informed consent and assent was obtained, with their mother present at all times during the discussions.

REFERENCES

Amaya-Jackson, L., & March, J. S. (1995) Post-traumatic stress disorder. In J. S. March (Ed.), *Anxiety disorders in children and adolescents* (pp. 276–300). New York: Guilford Press.

American Psychiatric Association. (1994). *Diagnostic and statistical manual of mental disorders* (4th ed.). Washington, DC: Author.

Breggin, P. (1991). *Toxic psychiatry*. New York: St. Martin's Press.

Charney, D. S., Deutch, A. Y., Krystal, J. H., Southwick, S. M., & Davis, M. (1993). Psychobiological mechanisms of posttraumatic stress disorder. *Archives of General Psychiatry, 50*, 294–305.

Frankl, V. E. (1984). *Man's search for meaning* (3rd ed.). New York: Simon & Schuster.

Levine, P. A., & Frederick, A. (1997). *Waking the tiger: Healing trauma*. Berkeley, CA: North Atlantic Books.

Roth, A., & Fonagy, P. (1996). Anxiety disorders III: Posttraumatic Stress Disorder. In A. Roth, P. Fonagy, G. Parry, & M. Target, *What works for whom? A critical review of psychotherapy research*. New York: Guilford Press.

Tieger, P. D. & Barron-Tieger, B. (1997). *Nurture by nature*. Boston: Little, Brown.

OTHER RECOMMENDED READINGS

Bettelheim, B. (1989). *The uses of enchantment: The meaning and importance of fairytales*. New York: Vintage Books.

Coles, R. (1990). *The spiritual life of children*. Boston: Houghton Mifflin.

Dodds, J. B. (1985). *A child psychotherapy primer: Suggestions for the beginning therapist*. New York: Human Sciences Press.

Doka, K. J. (Ed.). (1995). *Children mourning: Mourning children*. Washington, DC: Hospice Foundation of America.

Rapoport, J. L. & Ismond, D. R. (1996). *DSM-IV training guide for diagnosis of childhood disorders*. New York: Brunner/Mazel.

Webb, N. B. (Ed.). (1993). *Helping bereaved children: A handbook for practitioners*. New York: Guilford Press.

Ziegler, R. G. (1992). *Homemade books to help kids cope*. New York: Magination Press.

The Role of Play in the
Recovery Process

Carol M. Raynor

Through the arts, we try to transform not only our joys,
but also our tears and anguish, paralysis and fear, and
the unexplained and mysterious into images of strength,
clarity and control.

(Steinhardt, 1994, p. 217)

My personal experience in working with children in
Missouri after the flood of 1993 reaffirmed my conviction that
children gain some control over their lives after disaster through
play. Virginia Axline, pioneer in play therapy, developed the theory that repetitive play helps children cope with trauma and
change in their lives (Axline, 1969). Quite recently, Karen Olness (1999), a pediatrician with 30 years of experience working
with children who have escaped wars or natural disasters, has
emphasized the importance of play in refugee camps. The stress
relief afforded by play is a priority when working with children,
according to Olness, along with concerns for malnutrition and
dehydration.

THE FIRST HOURS

In the first hours after rescue—the emergency and rescue stage—the child's initial reaction is one of fear, primarily the fear of being left alone or abandoned. Children are absolutely dependent on adults for security, and they may feel complete panic. Most children will want to be close enough to caretakers to touch them and to be held. Play may be limited in these first few hours because of paralyzing fear. Having food, a place to sleep, and the warmth and proximity of loved ones are top priorities. In this time of roller-coaster emotions, a good listener is essential, someone to whom the children can tell the personal stories of their experience (Knuckey, 1997).

USING PLAY TO RESTORE ORDER

Play opportunities become increasingly important as soon as the children feel that they are safe and that a measure of stability has been restored. Play materials and space to play are extremely important in the relief phase, when refugees are in shelters. In the recovery phase, people are beginning to put their lives back together. Children are still reliving the terrors internally, and they need opportunities to play out the trauma with toys and art materials. Often adults expect children to stop dwelling on the disaster long before they have processed the experience thoroughly.

BASIC STRATEGIES

One should be reminded of some basic strategies in working with children in play situations. Sit down with the children, look them in the eye, and relate to them in ways that deemphasize your largeness compared with their smallness. Share in activities that focus on something outside the children as they begin to venture into the process of healing. Even a shy and acutely distressed child will usually participate in rolling or tossing a ball back and forth. Respect psychological space and proceed with relationships at the child's own pace.

It is essential to talk in a calm and soothing tone in times of severe stress. Beware of manners of expression that create barriers to effective communication (Gordon, 1970). False sympathy and reassurance are not helpful: "You'll feel better after you rest awhile, you're just tired." Ordering or commanding is equally ineffective: "Stop feeling sorry for yourself . . . you must not feel that way." Accept feelings as they are expressed. Do not try to change the child's statements. Do not argue or be demanding: "Just try to think about something else right now." Severe stress can cause children and adults to obsess about certain fears or ideas. Conversations should not divert them from the serious emotions they are displaying: "Let's play a game and forget all about this." Above all, avoid labeling children in negative ways: "You are too big to act like that, don't be a baby." Listen to yourself and think about how a frightened child would react to your words.

Look for the feelings behind the behaviors that you observe. The simplest assessment for negative feelings is to ask, "Are you feeling sad?" You can respond with simple statements such as "That sounds as if it was really hard for you." "You must be very upset." Resist the temptation to add, "Don't worry, everything will turn out just fine." It is helpful to say something like: "I wish I had some magic to bring your pet back to you . . . or to find your bicycle." Strive to be honest, but be very positive in your outlook.

Above all, be willing to address the instances of grief, loss, guilt, shame, fear, and danger stored in your own past. It is imperative to find someone with whom to share your feelings. Keeping a personal journal can help maintain a perspective. Debriefing your personal trauma in dealing with human tragedy is basic to your own mental health.

COME PREPARED: A CHECKLIST

A suitcase of appropriate play materials is an ideal way of having the ingredients for both free play and directed activities. Churches or community groups or the staff of hospitals can be challenged to assemble the toys. Small plastic bags can hold items with small pieces and liquid materials that could spill. A cloth bag with a drawstring is useful for storage. Hospitals often send home small plastic basins with discharged patients; these basins work nicely for water play.

United Methodist volunteers have used kits of play materials in Kobe, Japan, after the earthquakes; in Bosnia in refugee camps; and most recently in Zimbabwe, Africa. Play areas have been set up on sidewalks and inside shelters. In some war-torn areas, these centers have been the only places in which children of different ethnic backgrounds could play in peace. Creativity can be used in marking boundaries of a play area. Strips of masking tape can outline the space. Hanging a clothesline along one side creates a changing art gallery.

A battery-operated tape recorder sets the mood by playing lullabies, relaxing music for quiet times, and marching tunes and music for expressive movement. If you are going to another country, search for musical tapes that be fun for children and reflect the music of the country you are visiting. Old chiffon scarves can be purchased in used clothing stores; these scarves are amusing for kids to swish in time to music or to use for dress-up clothes. Make up silly songs. For example, to the tune of "The Muffin Man": "Oh, do you know the wind does blow, the wind does blow, the wind does blow? Do you know the wind does blow and it really scares me so!" (Miller & Weaver, 1997).

Fears at night are easier to handle if a child can hold a flashlight for a while. An extra supply of batteries is essential for the tape recorder, for a portable radio, and for a couple of flashlights.

Pretend toys set the stage for the imagination: two or three small dolls (ones that can be washed), toy cars, emergency vehicles, trucks, blocks, and puppets. Toys that suggest reconstruction activities and the restoring of order to chaos are important—a hard hat, plastic tools, a paint brush to use in painting walls (with water!), and work gloves in kid sizes. Building with blocks, tearing down, and rebuilding will give children a feeling of power and control. Puzzles give a sense of order as they are worked, putting things back together where they belong.

Art supplies should be included in a variety of media (see Appendix A): crayons, chalk, colored markers, rolls of plain paper for a mural telling the story of the disaster, purchased or homemade modeling clay (see Appendix B), containers of tempera paint and glue, cut-up sponges for painting, pen and pencils for drawing, glue sticks and small bottles of craft glue, scissors, paper bags and paper plates for decorating, yarn, stapler, and staples. Small children can spend hours painting rocks or gravel with watercolors. A banner can be created of words and pictures that describe the many feelings people are experiencing. Colored markers can provide a range of skin colors to use in drawing. A stamp pad can be created with a dab of tempera on a paper towel; each child can make a thumbprint picture. Perhaps an animal can be designed from the thumbprint. A wreath of thumbprint animals with names of individuals can be hung in the art gallery. A small washcloth and hand towel help in cleaning up.

The themes of drawings and imaginary play are often repeated over and over in an effort to get some power and control over the traumatic events. After the flood of 1993, one little girl again and again drew a picture of her trailer house floating off down the road. Just as scar tissue builds in layers over a physical wound, the repetition of stories told and played out seems to bring emotional healing (Gregorian, Azarian, DeMaria, & McDonald, 1996).

GAMES TO TRY

Volunteers can lead in activities in the center of a circle or can allow for free play. Tape-recorded interviews with kids can focus on unfinished sentences: "Everyone was so excited when . . ." "During the storm I was worried about . . ." "I would really like it if . . ." An add-on story using the tape recorder is also an interesting way for children to recount their experiences and use their imaginations as well.

Three-by-five index cards can be used in several ways. Duplicate newspaper photos of the disaster can be placed on cards, turned upside down, and matched in pairs in a game of memory. Feeling words (see Appendix C) and subject words (school, sister, brother, mother, father, dog, house, road, etc.) can be written on individual cards. Players throw dice and pick up as many cards as the number thrown. Making a sentence with the words earns 10 points; making a story earns 20 points. Feeling faces drawn on the cards can be used in a game that asks players to tell about a time when they felt the emotion on the card. An index card divided into four spaces can be given to children with instructions to write or draw in each square: my favorite person, how I look when I am sad, my pet, and someone I know who died. A reflective discussion can take place about the responses.

High-energy activities are good when children are confined in small areas. Relay races, obstacle courses, rhythmic dancing to music, and jumping rope are favorites. Emotions can be elicited by having the child throw a bean bag into a box and expressing feelings as he or she throws, saying "I get so angry when . . ."

THE HEALING POWERS OF PLAY

Fred Rogers of television fame has written some of his thoughts on play and coping. He points out that all of us have experienced painful events of the past which we want to leave in the distance. Sometimes these events jump out at us when we least expect them and become disturbing images in our present. It seems that when children talk and play in a way that expresses feelings, crises and traumatic events resolve and settle into the past more easily. Rogers maintains that learning to express feelings through play can make the difference between bending and breaking when strong winds hit us (Head & Rogers, 1986).

Play is the language of the inner world of the child. Children today tend to turn to electronic entertainment when they feel troubled. When disaster strikes, the old familiar ways of coping are not available. Child advocates, both professional and volunteer, need to be prepared to lead children into free play and directed activities that will help them express feelings and survive emotionally in times of emergency.

REFERENCES

Axline, V. (1969). *Play therapy* (Rev. ed.). New York: Ballantine Books.

Gordon, T. (1970). *Parent effectiveness/teacher effectiveness.* New York: McKay.

Gregorian, V., Azarian, A., DeMaria M., & McDonald, L. (1996). Colors of disaster: The psychology of the "black sun." *The Arts in Psychotherapy, 23,* 1–14

Head, B., & Rogers, F. (1986). *Mister Rogers' playbook: Insights and activities for parents and children.* New York: Berkeley Books.

Knuckey, G. (1997). *Pastoral care for children and youth in disaster.* Paper presented at Global Gathering III: Caring For Children in the Midst of Disasters. United Methodist Committee on Relief, Kansas City, MO.

Miller, V., & Weaver, B. (1997). *Spiritual and emotional care with children who have experienced disaster situations.* Paper presented at Global Gathering III: Caring For Children in the Midst of Disasters. United Methodist Committee on Relief, Kansas City, MO.

Olness, K. (1999, October 11). New handbook offers advice on aiding children. *The Kansas City Star*, A3.

Steinhardt, L. (1994). Creating the autonomous image through puppet theatre and art therapy. *The Arts in Psychotherapy*, 21, 205–218.

APPENDIX A

PLAY THERAPY SUPPLIES FOR USE WITH CHILDREN AFTER A DISASTER

Art Supplies
- Masking tape
- Crayons (two boxes)
- Colored markers (two boxes)
- Rolls of plain shelf paper for murals
- White paper (8 ½ × 11), 50 sheets
- Modeling dough (purchased or homemade)
- Sidewalk chalk
- Glue sticks and small containers of craft glue

- Cotton balls (25 in small plastic bag)
- Tongue depressors or craft sticks (25 in small plastic bag)
- Plastic gloves (four pairs of food-handler type in a plastic bag)
- Pipe cleaners (two packages)
- Small safety scissors (four to six pairs)
- Lunch bags (25)
- Paper plates (25)
- Pens and pencils
- Straws (25 in a plastic bag)
- Yarn (small ball)
- Paint brushes (small, ½-inch wide, 1-inch wide)
- Watercolors (two boxes)
- Tempera paints (small plastic containers)
- Cut up sponges for painting

Babies and Soft Cuddlies
- A small doll that can be washed
- Small animals and dolls that are soft, warm, and comforting
- Puppets (one soft and furry, one terry cloth for water play)
- Two small hand towels
- One small flannel receiving blanket

Toys for Pretend Work and Reconstruction
- Blocks
- Village mat (an outline of roads and a town; available in cloth or plastic)
- Sturdy plastic tools
- Hard hat

- Work gloves
- Cellular toy phone
- Little people, workers, and families

Quiet Games
- Puzzles (three or four in plastic bags)
- Books (three or four)
- Dice

Active Games
- Beanbags
- Inflatable beach ball
- Scarves (three or four)

Miscellaneous
- Small tape recorder with extra batteries
- Tapes of different kinds of music
- Stapler and staples
- 3 × 5 index cards
- Small unbreakable mirror
- Clothesline (12 ft) and 12 clothespins
- Flashlights (two, with extra batteries)
- Small portable radio
- Small plastic basin (hospital size)

Activities for Elementary School-Age Children
- Cards
- Balls
- Jacks
- Jump rope

Source: Miller & Weaver, 1997.

APPENDIX B
RECIPE FOR PLAY DOUGH

2 cups flour
1 cup salt
2 tablespoons alum
1 ½ cups warm water
1 tablespoon cooking oil
Food coloring—a few drops

Combine flour and salt. Add alum to warm water along
with cooking oil and food coloring. Mix liquids with dry ingredients. Knead until consistency is pliable. Store in small plastic
bags.

APPENDIX C
USEFUL FEELING WORDS

happy	frustrated
sad	determined
shy	guilty
discouraged	disappointed
proud	grieving
confident	worried
content	brave
angry	lonely
embarrassed	scared
surprised	excited

7

Group Interventions for Children in Crisis

Gordana Kuterovac Jagodic
Ksenija Kontac
Wendy N. Zubenko

GROUP ACTIVITIES SERVE MANY PURPOSES. GROUP ACTIVITIES can organize children's free time; create a supportive and comforting environment; encourage the healthy expression of emotions; provide for the sharing of problems and difficulties; encourage socialization with peers; and create opportunities for building confidence, skills, and knowledge. Many of these activities are related to play and expressive activities such as art, music, dance, drama, and writing. There are also specific activities organized for children with particular problems, such as aggression, poor socialization, grief, or loss of developmentally appropriate skills.

Because reactions to traumatic experiences are similar for most children, group interventions can be a real godsend when mental health professionals are overwhelmed by the number of children in need of assistance. Thus, intervention efforts of mental-health professionals and other helpers can be made easier in times when many children are in need of help. In most cases a generic approach is appropriate for the great majority of trauma survivors (Klingman & Hochdorf, 1993). The generic approach recognizes common patterns of behavior seen in crisis situations and emphasizes large-scale interventions that focus on the characteristic reactions and symptoms. These large-scale interventions include group interventions through schools, the community, and the media.

In contrast to an individual approach, in which individually targeted and tailored counseling or even therapy is implemented, the group approach uses advantages of group interaction to alleviate problems and stimulate the readaptation of children with similar traumatic experiences or reactions. Because children have a need to socialize with their peers, group work offers the best environment for a child's learning, for the development of social skills and self-confidence, for social networking, and many other aspects that are important in child development. In a peer group children can develop their potential; learn about cooperation, responsibility, and how to express feelings in a suitable way; and how to solve conflicts and overcome aggression. A group approach is an excellent way to focus on the *normalization* of the environment for traumatized children overcoming loss and grief.

PLANNING GROUP WORK WITH CHILDREN

The importance and effort of the planning phase are often underestimated by helpers. In our experience planning is one of the most important phases of group work. Planning influences the success of group work, the whole group process, and group leadership. Planning of group work with children should always include both planning of the group work process (the definition of the aims, methods to be used, and desired results of the particular group) and planning of each group session. Before deciding to establish a group of any kind, you need to plan where and when the group will be organized, who will participate, how the group members will participate, who will lead the group, for what period of time the group will run, and how the group will be materially and financially supported. Some groups will be organized as closed and regular groups for particular children in need, whereas others will be more open and attended periodically by a wider population of children.

If group leaders are paraprofessionals or inexperienced helpers, it is important that the sessions are planned and structured. This structure helps to provide the group leaders with feelings of competence, security, and self-confidence, which, in turn, improves the children's experience of the group. If group sessions are not planned, children often show insecurity, withdrawal, aggression, and tension. This leads to reluctance to attend and participate in the group, as well as an overall unhelpful experience for the children and the leader. Structure and preparation support an environment that children find more secure, safe, open, and appropriate for sharing. The planning and preparation of each session involve the design of the group process in detail, including timing, the list of activities, preparation of material and equipment, and other items that might contribute to the goals of the group.

Group Leaders

All groups described in this chapter can be led by paraprofessionals under the supervision of a professional. Paraprofessionals can be teachers, students of social work, psychology, or medicine, special teachers, preschool teachers, nurses, nuns, priests, volunteers, and parents. Whether the leaders are professionals or nonprofessionals, they should have at least a modest knowledge of the level of development of the children in the group, as well as some information about group interventions, before they begin. Leaders should be trained in group work, communication skills, stress and trauma, loss and grief, and child development.

When working with children who have experienced trauma, group leaders should have particular characteristics, knowledge, and motivation. The work is very demanding and requires much patience and good communication skills. Also, a genuine interest in this kind of work, as well as realistic expectations for both themselves and the children, is paramount. Leaders must be aware of their own thoughts, feelings, and behaviors in situations over which they recognize that they themselves have little control. They must accept their limitations in such situations and try to invest their energy in something they can do or they should refer to a mental health professional. It is important for group leaders to choose the group they will lead according to their skills and preferences. It is preferable for each group to have at least two group leaders who can support each other.

Poorly recruited or ill-trained group leaders can be the source of difficulties in group work. If a group leader is not motivated to do this kind of work, is not well trained, has been poorly prepared to lead the group, or is not skilled in forming quality relationships with children, he or she will lose enthusiasm for working with children. His or her change in behavior will discourage the children from participating and will have a negative effect on the group work. Regular supervision should be the duty and responsibility of each professional or paraprofessional, as well as of their organizations and employers. Supervision has an educative, evaluative, and motivating impact not only on the group leader but also on the whole program.

Parents

It is important to have regular contact with parents. Organizing regular meetings of the parents of all the children from the group will contribute to the overall quality of the intervention. Parents can discuss the questions they have about their children and obtain information about the process and hoped-for outcome of a particular group.

Regular contact with parents provides a great opportunity to help both the parents and their children in times of crisis. It is always beneficial if parents volunteer as coleaders in the group. Parent meetings can also be the forum for teaching parents better communication skills to use with their children, to help them improve their relationship with the children, to give them feedback about their children, and to obtain the parents' support for the intervention. Parent meetings provide opportunities for the parents to share their own fears, doubts, and worries about their child as well. This can help in the normalization of their own thoughts and feelings, especially if they can compare their own experiences with that of other parents. And psychosocial programs help to raise the awareness of parents about mental health issues and children's rights and thus improve their own parenting skills as well as their social and communication skills—all of which can decrease family violence and child abuse.

Motivating Children to Participate

Children should voluntarily enter and participate in the groups. In order to motivate the children and encourage them to participate, the activities should be interesting and attractive. It is more interesting if the leaders introduce group contents through the different sensory channels such as play, drawing, music, and storytelling. Group leaders need to be creative and inventive to help motivate a child to participate.

Children's needs also change over time, which requires changes to the group program, as well as adjustment of the whole group process. It is important to constantly monitor the group process and members of the group in order to react appropriately to the children's changing needs and abilities.

Who to Include

Ideally, all children are included in the group interventions. Often, however, this is not possible. It is important, therefore, to define the criteria for the selection of children for the groups. One of the first criteria to be considered is whether the child has preserved a basic trust in other people. Sometimes traumatized children have much difficulty trusting others, especially strangers, or they are very suspicious of others. These children require more individual attention than they can obtain in a group setting. With these children, it is better to first work individually and include them in groups at a later time when they are able to develop a trusting relationship.

The inclusion criteria always depend on the purpose and aim of the group. Members of the group can be made up of dissimilar members (heterogeneous). This mixture can enrich the group content and the group dynamics and contribute to variety in the group. On the other hand, sameness among group members (homogeneity) can lead to a better understanding of specific problems and experiences. It is not important whether the group is homogeneous or heterogeneous—most important is to establish a group that will function well (Buncic, Ivkovic, Jankovic, & Penava, 1994).

Space and Location, Where to Meet

The location of the group should be close to the children's homes or accommodations and should preferably represent natural, normal, and familiar places to the children. Most groups can be organized in schools, preschool centers, community centers, hospitals, shelters, or libraries. The group should always have the same space, day, and time for the group sessions. This predictability offers a stabilizing force in the children's lives. Group space should be large enough to accommodate chairs in a circle or the use of tables. Children need space to move, and many activities require body movements; therefore, the space should allow for moving chairs and tables aside.

The space needs to be pleasant and comfortable. Group members will bond not only to other group members but also to the place. It is important that the children feel comfortable and are ready to get to work when they enter the space. If possible, group members should participate and contribute in decorating and arranging the space (bringing pictures, wall posters, plants, etc.). At the end of each session children should tidy up the space together with the group leader.

Group Rules

From the very beginning, each group must set up group "ground rules." Establishing agreed-on rules will improve and strengthen group togetherness. Members of the group, together with the group leader, propose and discuss ground rules. The most common and basic rules in most groups are:

- *Confidentiality*. Not to discuss outside of the group what has been said by any member of the group during the group session, and not to disclose information about other group members.

- *Respect.* To respect other's thoughts and feelings, recognizing the differences among members and the uniqueness of each group member.
- *Consideration.* To think about members' thoughts, feelings, needs, by having the consideration to listen while one member is talking, and agreeing not to interrupt nor to shout during sessions.
- *Honesty.* To agree that there are no right or wrong, good or bad feelings. To be as honest as possible and to be as supportive as possible.
- *Safety.* To vow that violent behavior (either verbal or physical) will *not* be tolerated in the group.
- *Punctuality.* To come to group sessions on time.

All members must agree to the rules. Often older children are asked to sign a group contract agreeing to the basic group rules. Children should always be allowed to propose new rules and to agree to the consequences if rules are not followed.

Evaluation of Group Work

Evaluation of group work is the process of collecting information about the effectiveness and efficiency of the group intervention. This evaluation is necessary in order to determine whether the group goals have been achieved and to determine the quality of the program itself.

Evaluation is an important part of group work and its planning. In a group it is possible to evaluate each session, each phase in group development, the achievements and changes of a particular child in the group, group work as a whole, and the group leader's quality of work (Ajdukovic, 1997). Evaluation lists completed by the children after each session provide feedback to the leader about the child's experience of the group meeting. This can help the group leader to plan the next session.

EXAMPLES OF GROUP ACTIVITIES WITH CHILDREN

Educational Groups

Education and school are important factors in the recovery of children experiencing crisis or trauma. Through educational group interventions, children can learn new skills and behaviors, as well as gain knowledge. Most of the groups can be organized in schools, preschool community centers, refugee camps, hospitals, mental health centers, or libraries. Assisting children in mastering the school program is more than just increasing their ability to achieve better school marks and success. The goal is to assist the children in the socialization process, which will influence their social development, family interactions, and relations with their peers as well (Pavic, 1999).

Outside of school time, teachers, parents, friends, students, volunteers, and other helpers can do much to help distressed children. It is possible to organize groups for children who need assistance in mastering a particular school subject. Members of the group should be children who are underachieving in a particular subject, those who have a poor environment for learning, or children without parental support. During the sessions children can repeat what they have learned in school that day, receive further explanations, practice a particular subject, learn how to study, play interaction games, and exercise to improve concentration and physical stamina. All of these activities should be rotated several times during one group session.

The expectation of educational groups is to help children become more successful at school and master the skills necessary for that success. This success will be seen through better studying techniques and social skills, increased learning autonomy, and fewer difficulties overall in school achievement. If there is need, it is also recommended that an *open group* be organized for all children, in which assistance in studying different subjects is offered. In this open group, it is difficult to plan all activities in advance, but it is important to follow the school program. One of the important aims is to teach children *how* to study. If a group leader identifies a child with specific needs, it is appropriate to refer such a child for individual assistance in studying.

Creative Workshops
In creative workshops children can use simple things such as paper in different ways to express themselves. They should be encouraged to give their imaginations free rein, to manifest their ideas and emotions, thoughts and feelings, by using a variety of colors and shapes. Through this activity children cooperate by sharing tools, glue, color paints or crayons, and other material. By working together, the children develop fine motor skills and learn persistence, endurance, and patience. The content of the activities can be very different—from making objects from paper (origami), cards, kites, windmills, or boxes to creating a collage based on a told story or the characters in a story which the children have made up (Koscec & Stankovic, 1999).

Papier-mâché is a wonderful technique for a creative workshop. Children can make different decorative items of practical use, as well as toys, and in the process develop their imaginations and creativity. It quite often happens that children, especially small children, become impatient to finish the item. It can help if there is a finished item at hand so the children can see how their completed masterpiece will look. Smaller groups of six to eight children are recommended for this activity.

Children particularly enjoy drawing together, which helps them express their feelings and encourages adaptive coping skills. Ask children to draw whatever they wish, allowing them the freedom to choose the topic and materials to be used. Then ask the children to share with others what they have drawn and what feelings they have about the drawing. Unconditional acceptance of the child's feelings and expression through drawing is important. Do not criticize or object to the child's feelings or the expression of these feelings through drawing.

Creative Writing Workshops

A *creative writing workshop* is an innovative intervention for distressed children who prefer writing to talking. In this type of group the children can express their emotions and thoughts through writing, as well as the other activities and games the workshop may offer. Through writing children can increase their sensitivity to emotional experiences and better understand their own emotional reactions. Through creative writing children can also experience emotional relief through the act of communicating to a small group. Children can often begin to express their feelings through storytelling, and each child should be encouraged to tell or write her or his story relating what has happened to him or her and his or her family, home, friends, things, attitudes, value system, and beliefs. Many different topics can be used to stimulate children to talk or write about all the changes, experiences, and feelings in their lives.

Children can provide and receive support in the group, use active listening, and work through their negative experiences. In a group they can learn cooperation and communication skills and teamwork and learn more about themselves. In a writing and journalism workshop, older children can learn critical thinking and problem solving as well.

Before children can start to write about a topic, they often need a prompt or introduction that can be in the form of an unfinished story, a guided fantasy, a favorite comic, or a song. Introductions encourage the children to express their feelings and thoughts in writing, and after writing, the children can be invited to present their work in different ways—through acting, singing, playing music, or talking. Writing should be fun, challenging, and full of play, not a task or obligation.

This workshop can be used in school during language and literature classes, for a particular topic, and to normalize children's emotions and reactions after traumatic experiences. It is possible to devote one or more sessions to a traumatic or war experience. Children can hear that other children feel similarly and can realize that their reactions are normal and typical of others. It is also a great relief if they hear others talking about things that they find difficult to discuss (Delale & Suvak, 1999). Children should share past and present experiences, but it is important to talk and write about plans and the future and how they see the future for themselves and for others.

Drama and Puppet Workshops

In drama and puppet workshops children have the opportunity to express their emotions, imaginations, and creativity and to learn cooperation. In drama and puppet workshops children can improve their vocabularies, verbal and nonverbal expression, and communication. Drama contributes to the development of living in the present, to a clear understanding of roles in day-to-day living, to our relationships with others, to the free use of imagination, and to creativity in everyday living. Drama also improves children's empathy and understanding for others. In drama children try to identify with someone else and try to "walk in another's shoes."

Drama by its very nature is based on cooperation. During planning, rehearsal, and performance children learn a great deal about giving and receiving (Bezic, Hart, & Uzeloc, 1995). Playing characters from literature brings meaning to the situations enacted and helps children find meaning in their own circumstances. If it is decided to have a closed drama group, the entire program can be different. It is necessary to prepare different exercises for verbal and nonverbal communication, to discuss at length the drama the children would like to perform, to encourage them to write if they wish, or to create a whole drama from scratch. Each session can be devoted to one of these exercises.

Children often use family situations as topics for drama. During one summer program in the small town Velika Gorica near the Croatian capital Zagreb, children chose to prepare a drama about the family. It was impressive how they saw relationships among family members and how they could identify their needs. They resolved "bad and conflict situations" in the family, doing it in a very healthy and mature manner. They performed the drama in front of their parents, which led to an important opportunity for parents and children to begin discussions of thoughts, feelings, and behaviors. After the performance, many children reported that family members started to talk and share more, and thus each became more sensitive and open to the needs of other family members.

A puppet workshop is suitable for very young, as well as emotionally blocked, children. With very young children, it is preferable to use ready-made puppets or marionettes in the form of animals or invented characters, or even people from the children's lives (Ayalon, 1994). Puppet workshops, psychodrama, and role-play have many advantages. It is suitable for illiterate children, those with poor writing and reading skills, and for those who prefer nonverbal communication. Children can use pantomime, body language, and other expressive behavior (Durovic, Kacavenda & Marinkovic, 1999). If possible, it is beneficial to move children from a passive to an active role while they are working through painful experiences.

Before making the puppet itself, the children should be encouraged to select topics, as well as the methods of working together. If possible, use fairytales, children's stories, or an interesting topic as a stimulus to interest the children. It is very common to use unfinished sentences (Breger, 1994) to create a tale. When a child is finishing the sentence, he or she is expressing feelings and sharing experiences while playing. Eli Breger (1994) used tales to format questionnaires for children who have difficulty responding to structured interview questions. Traumatized children should be encouraged but not forced to tell a story. And a child should never be persuaded or forced to express or describe a traumatic event.

After the group has made its decision about the topic and methods, discuss the topic and the characters in detail. Once the puppets or dolls have been made, the children can play in the group with dolls, tell a story, play without sounds, or with music. Many possibilities exist for the children to express their thoughts and feelings while playing with the puppets. This play can develop into a puppet theater.

Visiting a puppet theater can be interesting for a group of children, offering them the opportunity for conversation with the puppeteers and all other persons connected with the puppet theater. Puppets can be made from very different and cheap materials (e.g., paper, pumpkins, wood, plastic bottles, cans, plastic glasses, and all kinds of packing materials). It is not necessary to organize and prepare a program for public performance. Participation in the workshop is sufficient reward in itself.

The objectives are to develop and enhance the imagination of the children, to encourage and create an opportunity for their emotional expression, and to allow them to gain insight and vision into the characters. In this workshop children also learn to cooperate and improve their skills in making puppets. Experience has shown that the optimal number of children in a puppet group is between five and eight.

Dance Workshop

Spending time with peers of the same age and developing rhythm and coordination of body movements are some of the goals of dance interventions. This intervention should provide pleasure in the physical activity of dancing as well. Each session should have a structure that is more or less replicated at all the meetings. Dance workshops consist not only of dancing but also of different interactive and socializing games, including learning about the body and getting to know one's own body.

Space for a dance workshop should be large enough to meet the needs of the group. If the space is too small, it is possible to practice dancing in two or more small groups. If there is a wide range of ages, dividing group members into subgroups according to age is also useful (Kusic & Osmak Franjic, 1999). Volunteers or group leaders do not have to be professional dancers. If a group leader likes to dance and can use her or his body to be expressive, others will join in and enjoy the group. Many children find this activity very liberating, and for many distressed children, it is great way for them to release pent-up energy, as well as to express themselves. Children should be encouraged to propose and create choreography together with the group leader.

Sports Activities

Sports activities provide a good opportunity for releasing energy and reducing stress if ground rules are set and maintained; the activity is organized and supervised; and, above all, safety is ensured. Sport activities are not an arena for violent behaviors, and violence cannot be allowed. For distressed children in particular, sports provide a good way to work off tension caused by stress and trauma, and through body movements, create diversion in order to ventilate thoughts. Through sports activities children can increase their feelings of control and understanding of their own bodies and thus strengthen their self-confidence and self-competency.

Team sports are popular among children, and sports such as soccer, basketball, volleyball, and handball are all suitable for leisure-time activity and do not require special equipment. The objective is for the children above all to participate and to learn the role of games so that they can become socialized with their peer group. Ideally, the group should not number more than 15 children (Mandic, 1999).

Begin each session with a discussion and agreement about the activity and the ground rules. The session has a structure like every other sports training session. Part of this activity is organizing friendly matches with other teams. Our psychosocial team organized sport matches for refugee children, and thereafter it became a tradition to organize football matches between teams of refugees in Croatia. Children who were not refugees joined in. Even when families returned home after the war, their schools continued organizing matches between school teams in the community.

Through sports activities children develop a sense of belonging to a team, a feeling of collective effort toward a common goal, and improvement of psychophysical abilities. For each individual sport, it is preferable if the group leader is a person who has trained in some sport. It can be a sports teacher, a student who is currently training in a sport, or a retired coach.

Socialization Groups

Socialization groups offer children help in gaining social skills through creative activities, such as games, parties, and sharing meals. Social development is a very critical part of a child's emotional health (Pruitt, 1998). Thus it is important to encourage a child to pursue activities that bring him or her into contact with other children of similar abilities, experiences, and interests.

Creative socialization groups are helpful for children who show certain behavioral problems and difficulties in functioning in stressful circumstances. Socialization groups have been shown to be beneficial for distressed children by helping them to overcome the usual hardships that are inherent in growing up, maturing, and getting an education (Jankovic, 1999). Often these distressed children are identified by teachers in the school as hyperactive, irritable, withdrawn, or aggressive. Many of these children are often involved in arguments and physical fights because they do not know how to resolve conflicts or reduce stress by using healthy and adaptive social skills. Other children with no specific behavioral problems can also benefit from creative socialization groups. And these children have a positive influence on the group as a whole by exhibiting positive, socialized, and healthy reactions and serving as positive role models for accepted and successful behavior.

Creative and interactive activities such as games, group projects, and group discussion are used to improve communication, social skills, and conflict resolution, establishing an atmosphere of cooperation instead of competition, emotional expression and relief, and healthy self-esteem and self-confidence. In this kind of open environment, children are able to express thoughts and ideas, as well as to discuss topics, under consideration, which not only inform them, but also provide relaxation and fun. Self-acceptance is a valuable trait to cultivate in oneself and to model for children. Through such activities children can learn and understand that everyone makes mistakes and can, in fact, learn from them. Groups of 6 to 12 children, aged 6 to 15 years, are ideal for such workshops. This is a long-term program.

Parent Groups

In parallel with the children's groups, parents should form their own groups. It is important for parents to share their doubts, fears, thoughts, and ideas about their families and children; to give and receive support; and to normalize their own experiences among parents in a similar situation. Activities should be designed to motivate both children and parents to join and to demonstrate and strengthen healthy parts of their personalities. In the first few group meetings popular and familiar creative and interactive games such as charades, Pictionary, and card games and activities should be used. In this phase group members get to know each other and build a relationship of trust, bond with each other, develop a group identity, and establish group rules that should be accepted by all members of the group.

Adolescent Groups

Adolescence is a time of considerable change in many areas of the adolescent's life. Ajdukovic and Ajdukovic (1998) found that the most frequent posttraumatic reactions among displaced adolescents in Croatia are bitterness toward people, irritation with others, loss of interest in activities, and restlessness. One can expect these reactions to have a negative effect on the adolescent's social relations and orientation toward life in general. School problems and an increase in the dropout rate appear as these adolescents grow older.

Adolescents who are living under difficult circumstances are more insecure, harbor feelings of guilt, have decreased self-confidence, see the world in black and white, and do not trust adults. There is more possibility for them to explore and to be engaged in risky situations. It is possible that they will develop more high-risk behavior in response to their feelings of futility with the passage of time. War and violence undermine many accepted moral standards. And in the face of this and in reaction to traumatic experiences adolescents will more easily express very risky behavior—neglecting school responsibilities, engaging in promiscuous sexual behavior, experimenting with drugs and alcohol, becoming delinquent, succumbing to eating disorders, and exposing themselves to risky situations. Educating adolescents about healthy behaviors is critical and should be integrated into an arguing group (Ajdukovic, 1993). It is particularly effective if other adolescents lead and conduct the group, helping peers to avoid destructive behavior.

Psychosocial activities can help adolescents to master social coping and communication skills, strengthen positive self-image and self-efficacy, increase self-confidence, compare attitudes in relation to a reference group, and discuss various topics specific to the adolescent population—all of which stimulates group cohesion and a strong network of social support on which they can rely to combat delinquency, suicide, drug abuse, and other high-risk behaviors.

Including adolescents in helping activities of any kind (to reach out to children, to act as coleaders in creative groups for children, to aid the elderly, etc.) is a good way to motivate them, to help them to feel useful, and to empower them. When working with adolescents it is important to adopt a tolerant approach, enabling the adolescents to direct and form their own activities (Pregrad, 1999). It is necessary to provide some structure but to leave the design and decisions about choice of activity and topics up to the adolescents. Adolescents have much to say and discuss, and they will do so when encouraged, respected, and accepted. Discussion forums are activities through which adolescents can improve their knowledge about particular subjects attractive to their age groups, which can stimulate creativity and personal growth, help them internalize positive role models and behaviors, improve self-esteem and mutual respect, and understand the importance of protecting of human rights.

Programs for Peace and Nonviolence

War and other forms of organized violence are themselves often followed by increased violence. There is a good chance that a child who is surrounded by violence will develop and grow into a violent adult. And even as children, these youngsters are not only victims of violence, but also often become perpetrators of violence (Uzelac, Bognar, & Bagic, 1994). After disasters and war, it is imperative that children are included in any programs that encourage peace and nonviolence.

The aims of programs for peace and nonviolence are to make children aware of the quality of life, to develop a positive self-image, to increase self-esteem and human dignity, to develop autonomy in behavior and learning, to teach responsibility for one's own behavior, to recognize problems, structure them, and creatively solve them, to improve communication and cooperation, to produce a better understanding of conflict as a process that can be productive, to develop the ability for nonviolent conflict resolution, and lastly to improve their ability to deal with emotions.

Teachers, students, and mental health professionals have been successful in leading such workshops, and it is fairly easy to include them in school programs. Such workshops have the power to change children's fear, shame, and guilt into feelings of self-respect, self-esteem, and trust toward other people, turning hate and fear into love and respect. Some of the topics covered by these workshops include loss, rage, prejudice, differences, belonging, conflicts, communication, nonviolent communication, cooperation, and human rights. Teachers report (Uzelac, 1997) that children realize during such workshops that trauma is a common experience for children in such circumstance. Once their experiences are shared, they find others like themselves and find the memories are not as bad as they previously thought—a sign that normalization of posttraumatic reactions has begun to occur.

SUMMARY

All the group activities described here have been used in work with children during and after war. But they are equally useful when implemented in psychosocial interventions in the aftermath of other types of disasters, as well as for the general prevention of risky behavior in children and young people. Only a selection of possible workshops has been illustrated here. There are a great many other activities that a creative helper can design. Helpers should bear in mind that recovery is a process and that the needs of beneficiaries change over time. Therefore, it is necessary to constantly monitor and evaluate the program and adjust it accordingly.

REFERENCES

Ajdukovic, M. (1993). Zdravstveni odgoj kao oblik pomoci traumatiziranim adolescentima [Health education as a form of help to traumatized adolescents]. In D. Kocijan Hercigonja, (Ed.), *Psihosocijalne pomoc Djeci i adolescentima, stradalnicima rata: pristupi traumatiziranom djetetu i terapijske tehnike* [Psychosocial support to children and adolescent victims of war: Approaches to traumatized child and therapeutical techniques] (pp. 31–33). Zagreb, Croatia: Institut za zastitu majki i djece, Komisija za kordinaciju pomoci i zdravstvenu zastitu djece u izvanrednim prilikama.

Ajdukovic, M. (1997). *Grupni pristup u psihosocijalnom radu* [Group approach in psycho-social work]. Zagreb, Croatia: Drustvo za psiholosku pomoc.

Ajdukovic, M., & Ajdukovic, D. (1998). Impact of displacement on the psychological well-being of refugee children. *International Review of Psychiatry, 10,* 186–195.

Bezic, I., Hart, B., & Uzelac, M. (1995). *Za Damire i Nemire: vrata prema nenasilju* [For Damire and Nemire: Toward non-violence]. Zagreb, Croatia: McMaster University and UNICEF Office for Croatia, Health Reach.

Breger, E. (1994). *Recovery program for child victims of armed conflict.* Zagreb, Croatia: UNICEF Office for Croatia, United Arab Emirates University, and Faculty of Medicine and Health Sciences.

Buncic, K., Ivkovic, D., Jankovic, J., & Penava, A. (1994). *Igrom do sebe: 102 igre za rad u grupi* [*Reach yourself by playing: 102 games for group work*]. Zagreb, Croatia: Alinea.

Delale, E. A., & Suvak, I. (1999). Writing and journalism workshop. In D. Ajdukovic & P. T. Joshi (Eds.), *Empowering children: Psychosocial assistance under difficult circumstances* (pp. 151–156). Zagreb, Croatia: Society for Psychological Assistance.

Durovic, M., Kacavenda, M., & Marinkovic, Z. (1999). Workshop for making puppets. In D. Ajdukovic & P. T. Joshi (Eds.), *Empowering children: Psychosocial assistance under difficult circumstances* (pp. 147–150). Zagreb, Croatia: Society for Psychological Assistance.

Jankovic, J. (1999). Creative socialization group for children. In D. Ajdukovic & P. T. Joshi (Eds.), *Empowering children: Psychosocial assistance under difficult circumstances* (pp. 185–198). Zagreb, Croatia: Society for Psychological Assistance.

Klingman, A., & Hochdorf, Z. (1993). Coping with distress and self harm: The impact of a primary prevention program among adolescents. *Journal of Adolescence, 16*(2): 121–40.

Koscec, A., & Stankovic, N. (1999). Paper workshop. In D. Ajdukovic & P. T. Joshi (Eds.), *Empowering children: Psychosocial assistance under difficult circumstances* (pp. 141–146). Zagreb, Croatia: Society for Psychological Assistance.

Kusic, D., & Osmak Franjic, D. (1999). Dance workshop. In D. Ajdukovic & P. T. Joshi (Eds.), *Empowering children: Psychosocial assistance under difficult circumstances* (pp. 131–136). Zagreb, Croatia: Society for Psychological Assistance.

Mandic, Z. (1999). Sports activities (Soccer training). In D. Ajdukovic & P. T. Joshi (Eds.), *Empowering children: Psychosocial assistance under difficult circumstances* (pp. 159–160). Zagreb, Croatia: Society for Psychological Assistance.

Pavic, B. (1999) Addressing school problems in adolescence. In D. Ajdukovic & P. T. Joshi (Eds.), *Empowering children: Psychosocial assistance under difficult circumstances* (pp. 175–184). Zagreb, Croatia: Society for Psychological Assistance.

Pregrad, J. (1999) Adolescents traumatized by organized violence. In D. Ajdukovic & P. T. Joshi (Eds.), *Empowering children: Psychosocial assistance under difficult circumstances* (pp. 83–86). Zagreb, Croatia: Society for Psychological Assistance.

Pruitt, D. B. (Ed.). (1998). *Your child: What every parent needs to know about childhood development from birth to preadolescence.* New York: The American Academy of Child and Adolescent Psychiatry.

Uzelac, M. (Ed.). (1997). *School-based health and peace initiative: Trauma healing and peaceful problem solving [Evaluation report]*. Zagreb, Croatia: UNICEF Office for Croatia, CARE, and McMaster University Project.

Uzelac, M., Bognar, L., & Bagic, A. (1994). *Budimo prijatelji: prirucnik za nenasilje i suradnju-pedagoske radionice za djecu od 6 do 14 godina [Let's be friends: Manual for nonviolence and cooperation—Workshops for children from 6 to 14 years old]*. Zagreb, Croatia: Slon.

8

Normalization: A Key to Children's Recovery

Gordana Kuterovac Jagodic
Ksenija Kontac

> When we came out from the shelter, we saw many dead
> people, and that many houses and buildings had been
> destroyed. We saw that there were no more trees, that
> the birds were not singing and that we would not go to
> school any longer.
>
> *Jasna, an 11-year-old, who spent 3 months*
> *in a shelter during the siege of Vukovar*

EVERY DAY FOR JASNA, AND FOR MANY OTHER CHILDREN
around the world, extreme events change their daily routines
and ordinary life, disrupt their psychological equilibrium, and
demand new ways of dealing with the social and physical world
in which they are growing up. Disasters, whether created by
humans or natural, can involve the destruction of homes, kindergartens, schools, and hospitals; can cause injuries and loss of
life; and can adversely affect large groups of people, not the least
of whom are children, who are one of the most vulnerable
groups in the population. Most important, disasters are out of
the realm of ordinary human experience and therefore capable

of inducing distress in almost anyone, regardless of earlier experiences or pretrauma functioning (Saylor, 1993).

In these abnormal situations, adults are often so preoccupied, and sometimes frightened, by their own reactions that they rarely communicate them. Children, in particular, are not likely to speak directly about their feelings and reactions, and sometimes they are even unaware that they are having them. Traumatic events cause a set of reactions and symptoms that are very similar for most children and adults. These include specific fears and anxiety; reexperiencing the event(s); avoiding stimuli and situations associated with the traumatic event; and increased arousal, which becomes evident in sleep problems and poor concentration, irritability, and hypervigilance. Children are particularly prone to separation anxiety, school-related problems, loss of previously acquired developmental skills, somatic complaints (stomachache, headache, etc.), and behavioral problems (Gurwitch, Sullivan, & Long, 1998). In communities that experience man-made or natural disasters, an increase of behavior disorders, family violence, child abuse and neglect, alcohol and drug abuse, and different physical and emotional difficulties are to be expected. Children and adolescents are at special risk because they lack experience in coping with trauma and stress.

The main goal of early interventions for children after a crisis should therefore be targeted to restoring, normalcy, a twofold process directed at (1) normalization of daily life and (2) normalization of emotions and reactions.

NORMALIZATION OF DAILY LIFE

Children who live in a predictable environment can more easily construct a personal representation of the world and the processes of life than children who live in chaotic and stressful familial or social circumstances. Consistency and unambiguity in daily routines and in parental discipline and control of a child's behavior and a low level of stressful experiences result in a high degree of predictability in a child's life. Children whose caregivers are responsive, affectionate, accepting, and approving will be able to attach themselves emotionally to those caregivers. These caregivers thus provide a safe base from which children can explore the world around them. Having a trusting relationship with an adult and a safe and predictable environment will help children develop a sense of themselves as worthy persons and a view of the world as a benevolent, understandable, and meaningful place.

Traumatic events in a child's life can disrupt or even destroy such ideas about the world and people (Tedeschi & Calhoun, 1995). For example, as witnesses to destruction and violence, children can lose the idea of their home, school, and community as a safe place and of people as good and trustworthy. This can cause a loss of security, which brings with it fear, anxiety, and horror. The words of Sanja, a 13-year-old girl who witnessed the wounding of several people, including her father and sister, illustrate this loss of security and hope for the future: "Ever since my father was wounded I have the feeling that the war will never stop, and that peace will never come. I believe that the war will continue and that we children will all be killed. I expect to live until I am 17. When I am 17 I shall die. The soldiers shall come and they shall kill us all with fire from the airplanes. I don't expect to live until I am 20" (Kuterovac, 1994, p. 116). It is essential to restore a sense of both physical and psychological safety in children following exposure to traumatic events. Without fulfilling that prerequisite, any interventions targeted at healing psychological wounds could be wasted.

Physical Safety

Physical safety is usually restored by removing children from the reach of disaster or trauma. Sometimes this can be very difficult to achieve—for example, an entire region may be affected by a large disaster where children can only be evacuated to less dangerous areas, not to entirely safe places. Evacuation, however, can be stressful in itself. For example, during the war in Croatia, children were evacuated from war-endangered towns, but their parents were obliged to stay to defend their towns. Children were therefore separated from their families and communities, which was additionally stressful for them. If at all possible, a safe haven should be found for children, and if possible, one parent or relative should accompany the child in any evacuation to a strange place. Everything should be done to restore order and daily routines.

Psychological Safety

Psychological safety is less easy to restore. One way of fostering psychological safety is to return a child, as soon as possible, to his or her pretrauma daily routine. Sometimes this is difficult because a child's home, school, or community have been destroyed or important people in the child's life are not present. However, keeping some routine is possible, even in times of chaos. These routines can include keeping contact with families people and activities. For school-age children, the most important routine is going to school and learning. For many children, school serves as a second security base outside the home. Indeed, children often spend as much time with classmates and teachers as with their families. In school, children can get additional support from their peers and teacher. During the war in Croatia, displaced children were immediately enrolled in schools in their new communities, or sometimes entire schools were integrated into other schools or established in refugee camps. In towns in which danger was prolonged for several months, radio schools were organized, with children meeting with teachers only when security could be assured.

School

Why is school so important for children who have experienced trauma or disasters? First, it is their most natural support system beyond the family, sometimes even the only support system when the family is dysfunctional or absent due to the disaster. Children usually spend as much time with their classmates and teachers as with their own families and view their teachers and classmates as important to their socioemotional, as well as cognitive, development. During a crisis parents are very often traumatized themselves and therefore not capable of responding to their children's increased needs. School also provides a unique setting for interventions targeted to help children after such events because a response through psychoeducational, teaching, and social activities in the school prevents "psychiatrization" of the situation and survivors (Klingman, 1993). Many psychosocial interventions are performed in and through schools and kindergartens, as well as other familiar environments in which children gather, such as libraries. Teachers and school psychologists are trained to recognize the symptoms of stress and trauma in children, how to identify the most traumatized children, and particularly how to create a supportive climate in schools. In addition, these professionals can be instructed in how to teach children who are experiencing decreased concentration, how to enable the expression of emotion, and how to give psychological support through themes taught in regular classes (Miharija & Leko Kolbah, 1994).

Teachers need to be trained so that, in times after crisis, they can adjust teaching methods to assist children in both mastering school programs and overcoming traumatic experiences. The teacher might explain new content using only very important data with many examples or use different teaching methods, such as different ways of presenting the material (e.g., visual, audio, tactile, and sensory; Pregrad, 1994).

Testing in school should be as often but as brief as possible. There are many ways of checking knowledge. We can ask questions verbally and in writing, but we can also ask children and students to prepare questions for a test related to a single topic. Children like to compete in groups, so the teacher can organize a competition of two or three teams in the class. One way to check knowledge is to ask children to give examples for particular topics. Different kinds of quizzes can be organized as a separate activity for children in their leisure time and can be used as a way of teaching in the classroom. It's best to choose one topic for each session with small rewards for winners, such as sweets, marker pens, toys, chocolate, notebooks, and so on.

Therapeutic teaching can also be used (Kerestes, 1994) for different subjects. Therapeutic teaching uses text literature to stimulate emotional expression, decrease emotional tension, and help to develop healthy coping mechanisms. Teachers prepare and plan a discussion after carefully reading a chosen text. During the discussion the teacher helps the children to understand their emotions and behaviors, thus strengthening their stress coping mechanisms. The discussion can be followed by drawing and more emotional venting. In therapeutic teaching, literature serves as a stimulus for structured conversation about not only the feelings and the experiences of the characters in the text but also those of the children. Conversations serve as opportunities to express emotions. These conversations can help children to better understand their own emotional reactions and the emotions of other children. Through analyzing the actions of the characters in the text, children can learn new coping mechanisms.

In order to prevent negative consequences of the trauma, teachers should work through particular topics that are usually found in school programs. It is important for children to learn about loss, their reactions, and coping mechanisms. Education about death can be one such topic. Loss and death are something that every child will eventually experience in his or her family, surroundings, and school. Through such education children can learn about different aspects of a particular topic. They can practice different ways of coping in stressful situations, particularly situations that follow loss and separation. Through education about loss and death, children can learn two important social skills: (1) the ability to receive support without feeling ashamed or dependent on others, and (2) the ability to give support without being over protective. These skills are important for furthering a child's emotional functioning. To educate about death, teachers can make use of poetry and prose, creative writing, and dramatic role-play, all of which will appeal to children's imaginations (Ayalon, 1994).

Teachers can incorporate short exercise periods into the school day, which will help the children relax, concentrate and feel energized. Children often enjoy "unusual" exercises, which they like to repeat. Sometimes children will use these exercises at home, teaching family members how to practice them.

Schools can also organize group activities for those children with increased needs, such as bereaved children, those with learning problems, those with heightened anxiety, and so on.

Shelters

Places of collective accommodation (shelters, refugee camps) are another important setting for interventions aimed at helping children during times of crisis. Children living in these centers are usually those who have lost their homes and, as refugees, are even more vulnerable than traumatized children whose homes and communities were spared from destruction. These refugee children not only have to cope with symptoms and reactions related to traumatic events but also must adjust to new life circumstances. The difficulties in adjustment can be expressed in many forms of behavior problems, such as difficulty relating to others, poor school performance, physical complaints, and longing for their lost homes, community, and loved ones. A child's dependency on the help of the community after losing everything can bring a sense of helplessness and hopelessness, which can lead to depression and anxiety.

After disasters, many displaced people live in hotels, shelters, and local government buildings (e.g., fire stations). Life in such places often lacks privacy and represents an additional strain to already traumatized individuals. These children have a great need for psychosocial assistance because they have been forcefully displaced from their homes, have often lost family members, or have been victims and eyewitnesses of the trauma. The various psychosocial programs and activities are used to normalize children's lives in order to prevent adjustment difficulties later on, to prevent the worsening of any mental health disorder, and to prevent the development of psychological disorders

(PTSD). Normalization also serves to help strengthen the individual and the family so they can overcome new or reccurring psychological difficulties (Ajdukovic, 1998).

Structuring Leisure Time

Life after a traumatic event requires much adjustment to a new life situation, and we often forget what an important role leisure time plays in a child's life. In difficult circumstances planned and organized leisure time has a great impact on the healthy adjustment and normalization of a child's life. The pattern of family life is severely disrupted for children in difficult circumstances, and parents are often preoccupied by their own problems and fail to recognize the children's needs for increased attention and support. To foster healing, the aim should be to create an atmosphere in which children can freely express themselves. Through different forms of play and ways of expression, children get to know themselves and their environment and develop new strengths and skills (Kacavenda, 1999).

Leisure-time activities should first of all give pleasure to the children rather than accomplish some task or result. Such activities can provide children with the opportunity to develop their potential, learn about the world around them, and share their worries with peers or adults. If the curriculum is personally meaningful, challenging for the child, and occurs in a stress-free environment, self-directed learning can be fostered as well.

NORMALIZATION OF EMOTIONS

Many reactions and symptoms that occur after traumatic and stressful events may seem very strange, unusual, and frightening for adults and children alike. Pictures and scenes of the traumatic event are often vivid and accompanied by other sensory experiences, such as sounds and smells. These memories can be very unpleasant and scary to children. They can interfere with the child's daily activities, particularly affecting the ability to concentrate and learn at school. Fears, longing, and emotional suffering can be so intense that individuals truly believe that they cannot withstand the pain and survive to another day. This can lead victims of a disaster or trauma to believe that they are going to lose their minds or go "crazy." Children are often so over-whelmed by their thoughts and feelings that they attempt to deny their emotions or to cover their feelings up. It is essential that care for children after disasters includes education about typical emotional and cognitive reactions and that the care provides opportunities for children to express themselves in a safe and nurturing environment.

Psychoeducational activities are very useful in achieving these goals. Psychoeducation can take the form of education workshops, public discussion forums, public lectures, pamphlets, media briefings, brochures, among other things. Psychoeducation provides basic information about the nature, signs, manifestation, and consequences of particular experiences, as well as different coping strategies that can help in such situations. Psychoeducational programs for children and adolescents help to prevent different types of risky behaviors (such as alcohol and drug abuse) and improve understanding of their own psychophysical development, needs, and behaviors.

Psychoeducation in the form of lectures and information is less frightening for children because it doesn't require talking about their own reactions, nor does it call for an individual plan for change. It is also very economical in terms of time and expense (Ajdukovic, Delale, & Druzic, 2000).

Personally more demanding, but also more effective, are peer support groups for children with similar reactions or experiences (e.g., for bereaved children, injured or handicapped children, children whose parents are missing, children with PTSD, etc.). Groups Encourage the exchange of feelings and conversation about similar experiences and reactions in a supportive atmosphere, which helps normalize children's reactions. In addition, children learn from each other's coping models and strategies, and can anticipate what reactions they can expect in the future. Moreover, because all members of the group share the same experiences, they trust each other more and can more easily accept all kinds of support without feelings of shame and stigmatization (Pregrad, 1996).

If children know what emotions and reactions are to be expected and are considered "normal" in traumatic or stressful situations, they will learn to normalize their own reactions and emotions. In addition, children may learn new strategies for dealing with particular problems and difficulties and should be encouraged to ask for individual treatment if needed. The efforts made to normalize children's daily lives, their community and homes, their reactions and emotions may sometimes seem banal and simple in comparison to interventions that include "real" therapy. Yet, for most of the children who are not severely traumatized, these interventions can be sufficient to free them from most of the likely symptoms that can affect children after trauma, helping them become the masters of their own future rather than prisoners of their difficult circumstances.

REFERENCES

Ajdukovic, M. (1998) Displaced adolescents in Croatia: Sources of stress and posttraumatic stress reaction. *Adolescence, 33*(129), 209–217.

Ajdukovic, M., Delale, E. A., & Druzic, O. (2000) Mogucnosti psi-

hoedukativnih radionica u razvijanju otpornosti djece [Psychoedu-
cative workshops in empowering of children]. In J. Basic, & J. Jankovic (Eds.), *Rizicni i zastitni cimbenici u razvoju poremecaja u
ponasanju djece i mladezi* [Risk and protective factors in development of behavioral disorders of children and youth] (pp. 261–274).
Zagreb, Croatia: Povjerenstvo Vlade Republike Hrvatske za prev-
enciju poremecaja u ponasanju djece i mladezi i zastitu djece s po-
remecajima u ponasanju.

Ayalon, O. (1994) *Spasimo djecu* [Rescue]. Zagreb, Croatia: Skolska
knjiga.

Gurwitch, R. H., Sullivan, M., & Long, P. (1998). The impact of
trauma and disaster on young children. *Child and Adolescent Psychiatric Clinics of North America, 7*(1), 19–32.

Kacavenda, M. (1999) The role of spare time in normalizing distressed
children's lives. In D. Ajdukovic & P. T. Joshi (Eds.), *Empowering
children: Psychosocial assistance under difficult circumstances*
(pp. 123–126). Zagreb, Croatia: Society for Psychological Assistance.

Kerestes, G. (1994) Terapijsko obradivanje literarnih tekstova u skoli
[Therapeutical analyzing of literature in the school]. In Z. Miharija,
& A. Leko Kolbah, (Eds.), *Pomozimo djeci stradaloj u ratu: Prirucnik za psihologe* [Help the children traumatized in war: A handbook for psychologists] (pp. 138–141). Zagreb, Croatia: Ministarstvo kulture i prosvjete RH, Zavod za skolstvo i Ured UNICEF-a u
Zagrebu.

Klingman, A. (1993). School-based intervention following a disaster.
In C. Saylor (Ed.), *Children and disaster* (pp. 187–210). New York:
Plenum Press.

Kuterovac, G. (1994). Zalovanje zbog gubitaka u ratu [Grief due to
the losses in war]. In N. Sikic, M. Zuzul, & I. Fatorini (Eds.), *Stra-
danja djece u Domovinskom ratu* [Sufferings of children in the Croatian war for homeland] (pp. 110–121). Zagreb, Croatia: Naklada
Slap i Klinika za djecje bolesti u Zagrebu.

Miharija, Z., & Leko Kolbah, A. (Eds.). (1994). *Pomozimo djeci stradaloj u ratu: Prirucnik za ucitelje* [Help the children traumatized in
war: A handbook for teachers]. Zagreb, Croatia: Ministarstvo Kulture i prosvjete RH, Zavodza skolstvo i Ured UNICEF-a u Zagrebu.

Pregrad, J. (1994). Oblikovanje nastavnog sata i samoaktivnost ucen-
ika, zadace i domace zadace [Creating of teaching process: Self ac-

tivity of the students, tasks and homework]. In Z. Miharija, & A. Leko Kolbah, (Eds.), *Pomozimo djeci stradaloj u ratu: Prirucnik za ucitelje* [Help the children traumatized in war: A handbook for teachers] (pp. 90–95). Zagreb, Croatia: Ministarstvo kulture i prosvjete RH, Zavod za skolstvo i Ured UNICEF-a u Zagrebu.

Pregrad, J. (1996). Tretman stresa [*Treatment of stress*]. In J. Pregrad (Ed.), *Stres, trauma, oporavak* [Stress, treatment, recovery] (pp. 107–146). Zagreb, Croatia: Drustvo za psiholosku pomoc.

Saylor, C. F. (1993). Children and disaster: Clinical and research issues. In C. Saylor (Ed.), *Children and disaster* (pp. 1–10). New York: Plenum Press.

Tedeschi, R. G., & Calhoun, L. G. (1995). *Trauma and transformation.* Thousand Oaks, CA: Sage.

Index

t indicates table

abandonment, linked with death, 93
abstract thinking, 115
academic achievement, 143–144, 166
acceptance, 121, 126, 145, 161
access, to disaster areas, 13
activities, 98, 143–155, 168, 197. *See also specific types of activities*
activity level, 109
adaptation, 76, 112
adjustment, 77, 166
adolescents
  avoidance in, 94
  demographic variables among, 20
  group interventions for, 153–154
  psychological development of, 86, 90–92
affection, 90
affiliation, 116. *See also* relationships

age, role in response to trauma, 75
aggression, 9, 16, 95*t*, 96*t*
  in school, 151
altruism, 40, 42
American Red Cross, 35, 64. *See also* Red Cross
  defusing and debriefing practices, 55
  publications, 60
anger, 41, 43, 95*t*, 119
anniversaries, 122
anxiety, 43, 116
apathy, 43, 99, 111
  among adolescents, 153
appetite, 44, 99
art activities, 31, 115. *See also* crafts; drawing
  supplies for, 128, 131–132
assimilation, 22
attachment, 78
audience, for publicity efforts, 26
autonomy. *See* independence
aviation accidents, response to, 66

Aviation Disaster Family
  Assistance Act of 1996, 66
avoidance, 38, 95t, 96t, 103,
  160
  among adolescents, 94
  of school, 43
Axline, Virginia, 124

Balkan conflict, 7, 16, 24–25, 31
battle fatigue, 35
bedwetting, 16, 42, 95t
behavior problems, 160, 166
  in wake of natural disasters, 9
belligerence, 96t
belonging, sense of, 42
belongings, loss of, 44, 50
bitterness, among adolescents,
  153
body language, 148
boredom, 116
brain, elasticity of, 113
briefings, 39. See also debriefing
Brofenbrenner, Urie, 74
burnout, 47, 58, 67

catastrophic event, 102
cathartic ventilation, 58
Catholic Relief Services, 13
certification, 65
child abuse, 160
child care, 66
children
  behavioral changes in
    preschool, 94
  concept of death among
    preschool, 93
  effect of loss of classmate, 8–9
  spiritual capacity of, 114–115
children's rights, 139
choreography, 150
chores, 108t

clergy, as group leaders, 137
clinginess, 94, 95t, 121
clothing, 106
Coconut Grove nightclub, 36
cognition, 78, 86
  disordered, 111
cognitive development, stages of,
  89t
collaboration, in data collection,
  29–32
combat stress, 35
communication, 11–13, 42, 45,
  51, 54, 97, 98, 108t, 109,
  155
  with agencies, 26
  barriers to, 126
  in group interventions, 138,
    145–146
  nonverbal, 148
  over-reliance on verbal, 115,
    116
  between parents and children,
    139, 160
  in school, 165
  terminology, 134
  through drama, 146, 147
communities, 32
  debriefings of, 58–61
  effect on interpretation of
    trauma, 105
  involvement in, 16, 17
  role in interventions, 41
community, role in interventions,
  15
compassion, 114
compassion fatigue, 47
competency-based orientation,
  81
concentration difficulties, 38,
  104, 160
confidence. See self-confidence

confidentiality, 59, 141–142
conflict resolution. *See* problem
    solving
consideration, importance in
    group interventions, 142
context, role in development, 74–
    77
control, 98
conversations. *See*
    communication
cooperation, 145, 152
    in drama, 147
coordination, body, 106
coping, 85, 97–98, 112, 130
    learning mechanisms of, 165
    models of, 169
    socialization and, 154
    spiritual aspects of, 116
    therapeutic teaching and,
        164
counseling sessions, 97
crafts, 17, 144–145
creative workshops, 144–145
creativity, stimulating, 154
critical incidents, 56
Critical Incident Stress
    Debriefing, 55, 56
crying, 16, 95*t*
cultural barriers, 20
cultural competency, 80
cultural diversity, 46
cultural sensitivity, 32
    role in interventions, 15, 18–
        23
culture, defined, 18
curiosity, 111
customs, 20, 21

damage assessment, 65
dance, 17, 149–150
data collection, 27–32

death, 9, 19, 103
    education about, 165
    effects on children, 10
    guilt over, 39
    level of exposure to, 20
    maturity and, 43
    preschoolers' concept of, 93
debriefing, 28, 47, 55–58
    case studies, 62–64
    community, 58–61
    handout for, 71*t*
defense-oriented reactions, 37
defusing, 53–55
    case studies, 62–64
demographic studies, 28
denial, 37, 93, 94, 168
dependence, 44. *See also*
    helplessness
depression, 43, 49, 116, 166
detachment, 104
developmental ecological
    perspective, 73
developmental stages, 10, 17, 73–
    77, 79, 85, 86, 107
diaries. *See also* journaling
    as data collection tool, 28–29
dignity, 155
    development in adolescents, 92
disaster mental health, 34
    training, 3, 14, 35, 138
disaster relief team, 47
    role in data collection, 30–31
disasters
    man-made, 7
    natural. *See* natural disasters
disaster syndrome, 36
discipline, 108*t*, 161
discussion. *See* communication
disease-based model of care, 81
disillusionment phase, 40, 41
disobedience, 96*t*

disorganized behavior, 95*t*, 103
displacement, 20, 21–23, 44
  fears about, 42
dolls, 132
drama, 146–149, 165
drawing, 145
  use in classrooms, 164
drawings, of traumatized
    children, 31
dreams, 38, 103. *See also*
    nightmares

earthquakes, 9, 10, 42
education. *See* academic
    achievement; public
    education; schools; training
educational groups, 143–145
educational handouts, 60
elasticity, 113
electronic entertainment, 130
emergency and rescue stage,
    125
emotional expression, 135, 149,
    152
  consideration in interventions,
    109–110
  stimulating, 164
emotional functioning, 37, 104,
    111*t*, 165
  restoring, 129, 167–169
  stability in adolescents, 92
emotional validity, 75
empathy, 10–11, 28, 51, 114
empowerment, of families, 81
environmental conditions, 76, 78
Erikson, E. H., 86
escapism, 112
ethnic bias, 19
ethnicity, 80
evacuation, 162
evaluation, of interventions, 27–
    34, 156

exercise, 106, 107, 108*t*, 165
  activities for children, 130
  dance as, 149
exosystem, 74
exposure level, 20, 60, 79
expression, 36, 97, 130, 167,
    168. *See also* emotional
    expression
  encouraging, 57
  through drama, 146
  through drawing, 145
  through writing, 145–146
expressions, facial, 109

fairytales, 148
families, 32, 75
  consideration in interventions,
    79, 80
  role in interventions, 16
  stability of, 72
  violence in, 160
family service, 65
fantasy, distinguishing from
    reality, 93
fear, 41, 93–94, 95*t*, 96*t*, 103,
    105, 160, 168
  associated with relocation, 42
  of blame, 64
  of mental illness, 45
  of night, 128
  of school, 9, 43
feedback, 102, 114
  in group interventions, 143
firearms, 8
fires, 9, 39, 46, 57
first responders, 56
flashlights, 128
floods, 9, 21
frustration, 41, 76
functioning. *See* emotional
    functioning; normalization
funding, 32

funerals, 56, 97
futility, 153
future thinking, 104, 146
  in adolescents, 90

gait, 106
games, 54, 129–130, 133, 152
generalization, limiting, 114
generic approach, 135–136
grief process, 19, 36, 41, 42, 50
  of adolescents, 20, 92–94
  cultural differences, 22, 46
  modeling, 52
grooming, 106
group dynamics, 61
group interventions, 5, 58
  activities, 135, 143–155
  choosing members of, 140
  evaluating, 142–143, 156
  leaders, 137–138
  number of victims and, 135–
    136
  participation of children in,
    139–140
  planning, 136–143
  rules of, 141–142
  sites for, 141
groups, in classrooms, 164
guilt, 153
guns. See firearms

hallucinations, 99
health-based competency model,
  81
helpers
  adolescents as, 154
  defined, 102
helplessness, 95t, 103, 166
  learned, 38
heroic phase, 40
holidays, 19, 39

homes
  as group intervention sites,
    141
  loss of, 9
homicides, 8
honesty, 52, 97
  importance in group
    interventions, 142
honeymoon phase, 40–41
hope, 114
hopelessness, 105
hormonal responses, role in
  effect of trauma, 106
human rights, 154
hurricanes, 46
hygiene, 108t
hypervigilance, 160

identity
  development in adolescents,
    90, 91
  displacement and, 22
  loss of, 28
images, 57
imagination, 120
  consideration in interventions,
    110
impulsivity, 78, 96t
income, and differences among
  adolescents, 20
independence, 155
  development in adolescents,
    90, 91
indifference, 96t. See also apathy
individual approach, 17
injury, 103
  from firearms, 8
innocence, loss of, 43
intellect, 111–112, 118
intelligence, 111
interpersonal growth, stages of,
  88t

interventions. *See also* group
   interventions
   determining best type of, 22
   evaluating, 27–34, 156
   how to offer, 50–53
   length of, 48
   principles of, 10–13, 78–81
   skills training, 14, 35
   versus therapy, 16
   timing of, 10, 38–39, 125
interviews
   with disaster workers, 30
   use in games, 129
irritability, 38, 43, 95*t*, 104,
   116, 118, 160
   among adolescents, 153
isolation, 44
   fears about, 42

journaling, 47, 67, 127
   and data collection, 28–29

lead agencies, 13–14, 30
lectures, 168
leisure time, 167
licensing, 65
listening, 10–13, 35, 51, 97, 125
literature
   searches, 29
   use in therapeutic teaching,
      164–165
local programs, developing, 14–
   15
local relief team, 15
   cultural diversity and, 22
loss, 9, 63, 85, 165
   of belongings, 44, 50
   consideration of types of, 112,
      113
   effect on adolescents, 92–94
   of identity, 28

management of, 113
multiple, 7–8
understanding, 121

macrosystem, 74
magical thinking, 93
mass care, 65
maturity. *See also*
   pseudomaturity
   death and, 43
meals, 107, 108*t*
media, 46, 51
   effective use by relief workers,
      23–27
medications, 49
memories, 38, 103, 121, 168
   consideration in interventions,
      112–114
memory, 118
mental health jargon, 45
mental illness
   family history of, 49
   fear of, 45
   symptomatic behaviors, 93
microsystem, 75
mobility, 106
moodiness, 43, 95*t*
   in adolescents, 90
morals, 153
   development in adolescents,
      91, 92
mortality, developing sense of,
   93
motivation
   of adolescents, 154
   of children in group
      interventions, 139–140
   consideration in interventions,
      108
Multiple Stressor Debriefing,
   57

musculoskeletal system, 106
music, in play areas, 127

National Transportation Safety
  Board, 66
natural disasters, 9, 10, 21, 42,
  46, 79
  stressors associated with, 16
needs assessments, time
  limitations of, 107
neurological responses, role in
  effect of trauma, 106
nightmares, 16, 95*t*, 103
normalization, 5, 37, 40, 58, 67,
  96, 98, 121
  activities necessary for, 107
  creative writing and, 146
  of daily life, 160–167
  of emotional functioning, 167–
  169
  of environment, 17
  group approach to, 136
  role of parents in, 139, 152
  signs of progress toward, 155
nurses
  as group leaders, 137
  as part of reponse team, 14
nutrition, 107

obsessive behavior, 112
open group, 144
organizations
  offering disaster relief services,
  65–66
  offering psychological
  intervention services, 64
outreach services, 51
oversight, 27

paperwork, 40
papier-mache, 144

paraprofessionals, as group
  leaders, 137
parents
  adolescents' perception of, 90,
  91
  communication with, 147,
  160
  as group leaders, 137
  groups for, 152–153
  involvement with children, 78
  reaction to trauma, 16, 94
  role in interventions, 81, 139
  separation from, 94
  stress of, 72
participation, 38
  in group interventions, 61,
  137, 139–140
peace and nonviolence programs,
  154–155
peers
  conflicts with, 151
  effect of cognitive processes on
  interaction with, 112
  in group interventions, 136
  influence on adolescents, 90,
  92
peer support, 67, 102, 162, 168–
  169
Pentagon attack, v
perceptions, reframing, 39
personality
  consideration in interventions,
  109
  development, 86
phobias. *See* fear
physical appearance, 106
physical examinations, 49
physical needs, 106–107, 108*t*
physical problems. *See*
  somatization
Piaget, Jean, 86

play, 130, 135, 167
    activities, 128
    areas for, 127
    basic strategies for, 125–127
    in group interventions, 139
    materials, 127, 131–134
play dough, 134
play therapy, 124
possessions. *See* belongings
posttraumatic stress disorder, 41,
        101, 102–103
    case studies, 117–122
    psychological needs of persons
        with, 107–114
    risk of developing, 57
posttraumatic stress reaction, 38,
        101, 102
    symptoms of, 104
posture, 106, 109
poverty, 76
prejudice, 155
preschoolers. *See* children
privacy, lack of, 166
problem solving, 98, 152, 155
    task-oriented, 37
professionals, relationships
        among, 7
protective factors, 77–78, 80
pseudomaturity, 111, 118
psychiatrists, as part of reponse
        team, 14
psychoeducational activities, 168
psychological development. *See*
        developmental stages
psychological distress, 103
psychological needs, of persons
        with posttraumatic stress
        disorder, 107–114
psychologists, as part of reponse
        team, 14
psychosocial development, 87*t*.
        See also developmental stages

psychosocial programs, for
        parents, 139
psychosomatic illness. *See*
        somatization
public education, 51
publicity, of psychological
        assistance, 24–27
punctuality, importance in group
        interventions, 142
puppet workshops, 147–149

quality of life, 155

race, 80
radio, 25
    schools, 163
reaction and recovery, phases of,
        39–41
reality, distinguishing by
        children, 93
rebellion, 111
recall, 103
receptivity, 105
reconstruction phase, 40, 41
Red Cross, 13, 23. *See also*
        American Red Cross
reenactment, 103
reexperiencing, 103, 160. *See
        also* memories; sensory
        triggering
reflection, 45
refugee camps, 17
    importance of play in, 124
refugees, 19, 29, 166
    sports activities for, 150–151
regional differences, in sensitivity
        to disaster, 20
regressive behavior, 42, 52, 95*t*,
        96*t*, 160
    in adolescents, 90
relationships, 78
    in adolescence, 91

among group intervention members, 141
with caregivers, 161
consideration in interventions, 109
group leaders and, 138
importance of spontaneity, 116
professional, 7
between victims and helpers, 104
relaxation, 107, 118
relief work, nature of, 48
repression, 37, 54
research, during interventions, 27–34
resentment, 41
residential settings, effect of trauma on adults in, 44
resources, use of, 53
respect, 142, 154
response team, 14–15
responsibility, 155
responsiveness, 161
retirement plans, effect of trauma on, 44
risk factors, 77–78, 80
  negative response to trauma and, 75–76
risk-taking behavior, 95t, 153, 168
Rogers, Fred, 130
role models, 98, 115, 154
  for coping, 169
role playing, 110
routines, 52, 96–97, 107, 108t, 113, 161
  in group interventions, 141
  and psychological safety, 162
rumors, 39, 46

sacredness, 115, 116
sadness, 105. See also grief process

safety, 108t, 125, 161
  importance in group interventions, 142
  physical, 162
  psychological, 162–163
  in sports activities, 150
schools
  avoidance of, 43
  firearms in, 8
  importance in normalization, 163–166
  involvement of, 112
  problems of traumatized children in, 104, 151, 153, 160
  psychological safety of, 9, 43, 162
  role in development, 75
screening, 49
scribes, 55
secondary traumatic stress disorder, 47
second disaster, 40, 41
security, 44, 97, 121, 125, 153
self-acceptance, 152
self-awareness, 102
self-competency, 150
self-concept, development in adolescents, 90
self-confidence, 110, 150, 152, 154
  development in adolescents, 153
self-esteem, 152
  development in adolescents, 92
self-expression, development in adolescents, 90
self-harm, 98, 99
sensationalism, 26
sensitivity, 26, 102
  in data collection, 27–28
  to trauma, 20

sensory triggering, 39, 56, 103,
    160, 167–168
separation
  linked with death, 93
  from parents, 94
  during war, 162
separation anxiety, 42, 160
sexuality, development in
    adolescents, 91, 92
shell shock, 35
shelters, as settings for
    interventions, 166–167
shock, 63, 105
sleep disturbances, 16, 38, 42,
    44, 95t, 99, 104, 160
  among preschool children,
    94
social isolation. See withdrawal
socialization, 44, 143
  activities to foster, 153–154
  in group interventions, 136
  groups, 151–152
  through sports, 150
social skills, death education
    and, 165
social workers, as part of
    reponse team, 14
Society for Psychological
    Assistance, 14
socioeconomic diversity, 46
somatization, 43, 94, 116, 118,
    160, 166
spiritual care, 66
spiritual needs, 114–117, 122
spontaneity, 110, 115, 116
sports, 17, 121, 150–151
Stafford Disaster Relief and
    Emergency Assistance Act,
    66
startling, 104
stigmatization, 16, 20, 45
storytelling, 110, 115, 145

stress
  acute, 16
  caused by poverty, 76
  levels and child behavior, 161
  normal reactions to, 34
  relief, 124
stress inoculation, 39, 55, 58
studying techniques, 144
substance abuse, 94t
suburbanites, versus urbanites,
    20
suffering, 105
suicide, 49, 62
  handgun, 8
Sullivan, Harry Stack, 86
supervision, of group leaders,
    138
support, 17, 145, 154. See also
    peer support
  giving and receiving, 165
support groups, 98
supression, 54
survival concerns, 42
survivor syndrome, 36
sympathy, false, 126

tantrums, 94, 95/it/I
teachers, 155, 163
  as group leaders, 137
  as part of reponse team, 14
  support of, 162
  training to instruct
    traumatized children, 164
temperament, 75, 78, 108
tension, 104
  release through sports, 150
testing, in schools, 164
therapeutic teaching, 164
thoughts
  obsessive, 126
  recurrent, 38
thumb sucking, 42, 95t

tics, 16
timeline reviews, 113
tolerance, 154
trackers, 55
traditions, importance during
    late adolescence, 92
training
    of group leaders, 138
    intervention workers, 3, 14,
        35, 65
    of teachers, 164
transactional principles, 77
transformation, 105
trauma
    common reactions to, 42
    defined, 102
    heterogeneity of, 72
    levels of exposure to, 20, 60,
        79
    psychological, 6, 7–10
triage, 48–50
trust, 140, 155, 161

unemployment, 76
United States, demographics, 21t
urbanites, versus suburbanites, 20
U.S. Agency for International
    Development, 13

Veterans of Foreign Wars, 23
victimization, 41
victims
    primary and secondary level,
        37
    versus subjects, 28

violence
    community, 72, 76, 78
    ecological model of, 76
    effect on children, 154
    family, 160
    in sports, 150
vocabulary, 146
volunteer agencies. See
    organizations
volunteers, 35
    as group leaders, 137
    training, 65

war, 7
weeping. See crying
wellness
    principles of, 106–107
    promoting, 105, 121
wet cement theory, 38
will, consideration in
    interventions, 108–109
withdrawal, 16, 37, 95t, 99,
        104, 116
    among adolescents, 94
    group participation and,
        137
    in school, 151
working conditions, for disaster
    relief workers, 66–67
World Trade Center attack, v
World War I, 35
writing, 145–146, 165

YMCA, 23